Games for Motor Learning

Ronald Dienstmann

Human Kinetics

Library of Congress Cataloging-in-Publication Data

Dienstmann, Ronald, 1962-
  Games for motor learning / Ronald Dienstmann.
    p. cm.
  Includes index.
  ISBN-13: 978-0-7360-7417-9 (soft cover)
  ISBN-10: 0-7360-7417-1 (soft cover)
  1. Physical education for children--Study and teaching (Elementary)--United
States. 2. Games--Study and teaching (Elementary)--United States. 3. Motor
learning. 4. Group work in education--United States. I. Title.
  GV443.D52 2008
  613.7'042--dc22

                                        2008022643
  ISBN-10: 0-7360-7417-1
  ISBN-13: 978-0-7360-7417-9

Acquisitions Editor: Scott Wikgren; **Developmental Editor:** Anne Hall; **Assistant Editor:** Cory Weber; **Copyeditor:** Patsy Fortney; **Proofreader:** Darlene Rake; **Indexer:** Dan Connolly; **Permission Manager:** Martha Gullo; **Graphic Designer:** Fred Starbird; **Graphic Artist:** Kim McFarland; **Cover Designer:** Keith Blomberg; **Photographer (cover):** Jason Allen; **Photographer (interior):** © Human Kinetics; **Photo Asset Manager:** Laura Fitch; **Visual Production Assistant:** Joyce Brumfield; **Photo Office Assistant:** Jason Allen; **Art Manager:** Kelly Hendren; **Illustrator:** Keri Evans; **Printer:** Versa Press

Printed in the United States of America   10   9   8   7   6   5   4   3   2   1

Human Kinetics
Web site: www.HumanKinetics.com

United States: Human Kinetics
P.O. Box 5076
Champaign, IL 61825-5076
800-747-4457
e-mail: humank@hkusa.com

Canada: Human Kinetics
475 Devonshire Road Unit 100
Windsor, ON N8Y 2L5
800-465-7301 (in Canada only)
e-mail: info@hkcanada.com

Europe: Human Kinetics
107 Bradford Road
Stanningley
Leeds LS28 6AT, United Kingdom
+44 (0) 113 255 5665
e-mail: hk@hkeurope.com

Australia: Human Kinetics
57A Price Avenue
Lower Mitcham, South Australia 5062
08 8372 0999
e-mail: info@hkaustralia.com

New Zealand: Human Kinetics
Division of Sports Distributors NZ Ltd.
P.O. Box 300 226 Albany
North Shore City
Auckland
0064 9 448 1207
e-mail: info@humankinetics.co.nz

*To Edgar Hoff, my middle school physical education teacher,
for his dedication and exemplary demeanor,
quietly showing us the path to, and the meaning of,
being a gentleman.*

*And to Elio Becker, my college swimming professor,
mentor, and great friend, for his continual search
for the highest standards of teaching.*

Thank you, Elio and Edgar.

Contents

Activity Finder

Games and activities in this finder are arranged by increasing complexity and physical intensity. The following list briefly explains the four categories used to differentiate the games and activities. These categories are discussed in further detail throughout the book.

Cooperative learning—Playing with each other, not against

Schema theory—High variability of execution within the assigned skill

Brain research—Voluntary movement exploration; low mental stress

Fun workouts—Games that provide active and engaging physical activity

111 Games and activities for motor learning	Cooperative learning	Schema theory	Brain research	Fun workouts	Page number
LOCOMOTOR SKILLS					
Rock and Talk	X				32
Safe Indoor Running	X				33
Marshmallow Hike		X	X		34
10 Ways to Cross		X	X		35
Want a Bus Ride?	X	X			36
My Happy Feet		X	X		37
Spinning Stars	X				38
Guide and Traveler	X		X		39
Crazy Trains	X	X			40
Wild Horses				X	42
The Bug Game	X	X			43
Zoo Tag		X		X	44
Running Feast		X	X		46
Mission to Mars		X			47
Jumping Land		X	X		48

111 Games and activities for motor learning	Cooperative learning	Schema theory	Brain research	Fun workouts	Page number
Super Hoopers				X	88
Blup-Up	X	X			90
Balloon Blup-Up	X	X			91
Up and Running	X			X	92
Half a Dozen Eggs	X				94
Throwing Sevens		X	X		96
Tap and Drop	X			X	98
Shooting Stars		X		X	99
Frisbee Hunt				X	100
Keep Them Moving	X	X			102
Keep It Clean		X		X	103
Soccer Stop and Dribble		X		X	104
Nutmegs				X	105
Caveman Soccer				X	106
Cross Fire				X	108
Mega Soccer				X	110
Extreme Soccer		X		X	112
Tag Pass				X	113
Scramble Tag		X		X	114
Chicken Noodle		X		X	115
One Bounce	X	X			116
Dribbling Warm-Up		X			117
Dribble Tag		X		X	118
Watch That Color		X		X	120
BasketBoom	X				121
10 Seconds of Life				X	122
Inclusive Basketball	X				124
Togeth'air Ball	X				126
Foot Tag				X	127

(continued)

Acknowledgments

I would like to thank the community of Topsfield for the opportunity it gave me to grow as a teacher at Steward Elementary School.

Thanks, Carol, for your unconditional support.

Thanks to my parents, Arno and Hedy, for being invaluable examples.

Thank you, Lori Greenslade, for your editing and support. Also thanks to Roseanne Felago, Shawna Warre, and Debbie Hale for their input on preparing the manuscript.

Thanks to Richard A. Schmidt for the exchanges throughout the years that helped me understand the schema theory.

At Human Kinetics, thanks to Scott Wikgren for believing in this book and to Anne Hall for her invaluable help in bringing it all together.

And to all the kindergarteners who never fail to remind me that "you're the best gym teacher we ever had!"

Introduction

Games for Motor Learning features a theory of motor learning followed by games and motor development activities built on this theory. The book combines Schmidt's schema theory of discrete motor skill learning (1975), cooperative learning, and brain research on emotions and learning into a unified approach to the teaching of physical education. This approach helps children develop fundamental movement abilities through active and inclusive games that create a socially and emotionally constructive atmosphere appropriate for learning.

This book provides an array of "Monday-morning" quick solutions; you can just open to a page, choose a tried-and-true game, and have a successful lesson to offer to your students. More important, though, Games for Motor Learning explains the theoretical background of this approach to teaching to help you develop your own lesson plans and successful games.

During the past eight years as a physical education teacher at Steward Elementary School in Topsfield, Massachusetts, I have witnessed the tremendous beneficial effect on my students of the approach espoused in this book. While my students participate actively and joyfully in every lesson, I gain insight into their emotional responses during exercise. This approach also helps me understand the brain states most beneficial for learning, memorization, and full enjoyment of the activities, and ultimately, the outcome for physical and psychological performance.

THREE CONCEPTS

I developed this approach to teaching while working for nearly a decade as a swimming coach and teacher with my then-university professor, Elio Becker (a former freestyle South American record holder), at his Golfinho Rehabilitation and Swimming Center in Brazil. I will never forget my first day reporting for teaching during my freshman year in college. I had no idea that I was going to have so much fun. To say that we tossed children like little rockets across the pool, making them fly over the water, after which they would dive with their hands together and chins nicely tucked in, gives only a small picture of the amazing variety of movement experiences the children enjoyed in Mr. Becker's hands. They were taught to spin, twist, roll back, roll forward, swim vertically, imitate all kinds of swimming animals, go through underwater obstacle courses, swim backward with one arm straight up above the water, with one leg bent up, and mix up movements from various styles. Mr. Becker always gave priority to children being highly skilled in the water before trying to teach or refine the mechanics of a stroke or concentrate on technique. The vast majority of our swimmers were literally fish in water.

I learned from Mr. Becker that motor learning can be extremely fun—full of laughs and screams of excitement—yet, the activities causing all this pleasure were utterly purposeful. There was a strong reason for having the children perform the most unthinkable movements and skills in the water. Mr. Becker spoke often of the need to feel the water, of having a strong sense of the resistance of water against hands and legs. Most of all, we worked on technique only when the children were definitely ready—when they were highly skilled and could focus on the technique without any other concern or fear. By then, their minds were at ease. They were confident and eager to be swimmers. We had cultivated in them a *voluntary* predisposition to learn and face challenges. This is an important factor in the approach described in this book.

Mr. Becker used this teaching philosophy all the way to training nationally competing athletes. Our swimmers always had amazing body symmetry in the water, and the majority developed almost flawless technique in their preferred strokes, even if they were not strong enough to be champions. Although not particularly familiar with Richard Schmidt's schema theory, Mr. Becker was intuitively applying it by constantly varying practice. Keep in mind the issue of variability of practice as you explore the approach to teaching motor skills in this book. This feature, which stems from Schmidt's theory, combines logically with current brain research on emotions and learning, as well as with the philosophy of cooperative learning.

Over the past decade, I have become intrigued with the role emotions play in learning and performance, with the effect of stress on our ability to focus and retain knowledge, and specifically with the so-called fight-or-flight state. Having been very interested in learning the intricacies of cooperative learning, I noticed that I could naturally combine these three topics—Schmidt's schema theory, cooperative learning, and the research on emotions and learning—into one sensible and functional approach to teaching and developing my curriculum in physical education.

TRIED-AND-TRUE INCLUSIVE GAMES

Part II of this book offers games that are active, entertaining, safe, and inclusive. These games do a better job of helping students improve balance as well as manipulative, locomotor, and social skills than the customary progressions of skills, which are often not emotionally engaging enough for the everyday gym class.

I use the fundamental movement abilities list (walking, running, jumping, catching, throwing, and kicking) developed by Indiana University professor David Gallahue (Gallahue, 1976). These six skills can be viewed as the "bricks and mortar" from which every activity in this book is formed, whether applying the schema theory or cooperative learning, or expounding on my understanding of what a brain-compatible game or motor development activity might be.

Fundamental movement abilities, as the name implies, are basic skills involved in the majority of childhood games and sports. Others skills could be added to this list, such as rolling, crawling, hitting, and twisting; however, for the sake of practicality, I have maintained these six movement building blocks.

Part II is the result of hours spent developing each game or modifying existing ones to fit the approach espoused in this book.

References

Gallahue, David L. 1976. *Motor Development and Movement Experiences for Young Children*. John Wiley and Sons, New York, N.Y.

Schmidt, Richard A. 1975, July. "A Schema Theory of Discrete Motor Skill Learning," *Psychological Review*, Vol. 82, No. 4, 225-260.

THEORY
LEADING TO
PRACTICE

CHAPTER

1

Schema Theory, Cooperative Learning, and Brain Research

Children need time, opportunity, and optimal conditions for experimenting with motor learning. Physical education lessons should be fun and diverse, not specialized and mentally exhausting.

An interest in the role of children's emotional states during the learning process led me to investigate the exciting field of cognitive sciences, in particular the part played by emotions, stress, and more specifically the so-called fight-or-flight state, during physical activities. Negative experiences in organized sports have been cited as the leading cause for some children's giving up sports; up to 67 percent of American children drop out of sports between the ages of 7 and 18 (Brady, 2004).

I relate the issues of emotions and stress to Schmidt's schema theory of discrete motor skill learning (1975), which is defined later in this chapter, to develop a program for teaching motor skills to young children in a stress-free, noncompetitive environment to maximize their learning and their enjoyment of physical activity.

The emotional experience attached to an activity is what makes that activity "brain based" or "brain compatible" or "calisthenics for the brain"—or any expression that suggests that it is good for the brain. However, the activity itself is not actually brain compatible. Rather, the mental state that the activity creates—as a result of a chemical release in the brain—is what makes that activity most suitable for learning. I will elaborate on this proposition later in this chapter.

Cooperative learning is the philosophical and pedagogical pillar on which most of the games in this book are built. Cooperative learning is a vast subject that has been defined and developed by many authors. I have particularly benefited from several books and articles on the subject by Johnson, Johnson, and Holubec. The writings of Erik Erikson on group identity also convinced me to adopt the cooperative learning philosophy into my teaching many years ago. Running the risk of oversimplification, I define cooperative learning—as it relates to physical education—as *children playing with, not against, each other.*

My study of the schema theory, brain research, and cooperative learning came together in what is a sensible pedagogical and philosophical approach to helping early elementary school children become *physically nimble* and *mentally comfortable* in sports and recreation. Cooperative learning, brain research on emotions and learning, and the schema theory form the triad from which I have built *Games for Motor Learning.* Part I explains the connection among these three concepts and the resulting pedagogy.

SCHEMA THEORY OF DISCRETE MOTOR SKILL LEARNING

Understanding the connections among the schema theory of discrete motor skill learning (schema theory), cooperative learning, and brain research on emotions is the key to understanding the games that are presented in the second part of this book. More important, such an understanding will give you the insights needed in order to develop your own yearly program of activities and games based on this approach. The following statement conceptually summarizes the connection of schema theory, cooperative learning, and brain research.

> **H**ighly variable movement experiences encourage cooperative learning. The resulting low mental stress enhances learning, enjoyment, and long-term retention of motor skills, according to current research on the brain.

This statement represents the nucleus around which the theory and activities in this book revolve. To clarify the preceding statement, I present an overview of the schema theory in this section, with particular emphasis on one aspect—exploring the many ways a skill can be executed.

The schema theory implies the idea of an internal mental guideline, or schema—a basic set of mechanical rules providing a jump start, a rough pathway to the execution of any number of variations on a skill. Imagine all the possible variations of any particular skill—for example, hitting a tennis ball. We would never be able to enjoy a tennis match in the short duration of a lifetime if we had to thoroughly learn and practice every potential way to hit an oncoming ball with a tennis racket. If, at this point, we agree that you and I would probably never be able to face each other on the court if that were the case, we must also agree that some kind of general guideline that rules "hands holding a racket and hitting a ball" must exist.

This mental guideline, this schema, encompassing the overall task of hitting a ball with a racket is developed by many opportunities of practice and experience, enabling a person to perform several modified forms of the skill that she has never tried before. The more variations of the "hitting" skill class there are (hitting from many different body positions, at various speeds, from different directions, etc.), the stronger the schema formation will be. In sum, the schema theory suggests the existence of a motor program that is strengthened by a variability of practice for a particular skill class. This comprehensive mental guideline, or schema, enables people

My Favorite Trick, page 79.

to perform endless variations of a skill based on a connection of factors from their previous attempts (These factors are discussed in greater detail on the following page.) A good example of a game with limitless possibilities that children love to explore is called "My Favorite Trick." The full game can be found on page 79.

SCHMIDT'S SCHEMA THEORY

Richard A. Schmidt proposed his schema theory of discrete motor skill learning in 1975 at a national meeting of the North American Society for the Psychology of Sport and Physical Activity. Although the idea of a schema as a "characteristic of some population of objects [consisting] . . . of a set of rules serving as instructions for producing a population prototype" (Schmidt, 1975, p. 233) was not a new concept, within eight years of Schmidt's publication, the theory received enough citations to be honored as a "Citation Classic" by the Institute for Scientific Information (Sherwood and Lee, 2003).

The schema theory accounts for discrete (distinct) actions, meaning movements of very short duration—for instance, a kick, a throw, or a jump. "Hence, continuous actions, such as steering a car or juggling, which are both of longer duration (allowing time for response-produced feedback to have a role) and more based on the performer's interactions with the environment, were outside the area of the schema theory" (Schmidt, 2003, p. 367).

Variable movement in a group game fosters cooperative learning.

Certainly, one of the most important proposals in schema theory is the idea of the motor program. However, "what's interesting about this work is that it links prediction of the consequences of action with memory of past consequences, without reducing movement either to a simple chain of packaged reflexes or the simple execution of a centralized motor program," wrote neuroscience author Alain Berthoz (2000, p. 18). A generalized motor program develops during the execution of an action of the same class (i.e., a movement that belongs to a common type such as jumping, throwing, or catching). The program is *not* the result of a specific record of movements, but rather of the connection (relationship) of the following factors:

> *Initial conditions* are the state of a person's muscular system, the position of the limbs and body in space, visual and auditory conditions, and the state of the environment before attempting the movement.

> *Response specifications* are the speed of, force of, and time used during the execution.

> *Sensory consequences* are sensory information received as feedback from eyes, ears, and proprioceptors during the execution of a movement.

> *Response outcome* is the last information input to aid the development of a schema, or generalized motor program, and is the actual outcome of the movement. The final execution of the movement may be different from what was originally planned. The latter is what is recorded in connection with the preceding three aspects.

Repeated attempts at a movement of the same general class strengthen the relationship of these four sources of information, and consequently, the formation of a schema, which in turn facilitates the future performance of variations of that movement. Note that the use of the term *repeated*

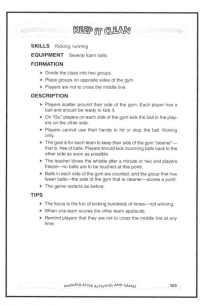

Keep It Clean, page 103.

attempts does not imply that the movements have to resemble each other exactly.

In the game Keep It Clean (found on page 103), the skill to be used is kicking. Whenever competition is involved, the criterion should be that every student, regardless of performance level, should be able to participate in the activity fully and have an equal shot at succeeding.

For any movement of a general class, performing the greatest number of variations will diversify the quality of the previously stated variables (initial conditions, response specifications, sensory consequences, and response outcome) and strengthen the schema. Variability of practice is discussed in the next pages.

One of the primary conclusions of Schmidt, as well as the many authors who have written in support of his theory, is that people are able to carry out movements belonging to a particular class (e.g., throwing) that they have not previously executed. Consider the soccer player kicking a ball under all imaginable game conditions and from an infinite number of body positions thanks to a generalized motor program (schema) for kicking that he has developed throughout a lifetime of playing.

Someone refuting the schema theory may state that the brain records or develops a neuronal pathway for each variation of each skill when performing it. A counterargument would be that the person may have never before performed, and will probably never again perform, a given variation in the same manner, under the same initial conditions, using the same response specifications, and resulting in the same sensory consequences; yet, she is capable of repeating the skill with certain differences. In other words, there is not a neuronal pathway for each variation, but rather a generalized program from which a blueprint may be tapped. This initiating generalized program is based on the storage of relationships on previous attempts of that class of movements—which is the essence of the schema theory.

In his original article, Schmidt wrote this: "It has seemed clear to investigators for many years . . . that when we make a motor response in a game, for example, we do not execute the movement exactly as we have made it before, and this is borne out by recent biomechanical analyses of movements. . . . If the response is to be programmed, for example, the sequence of muscle commands would be appropriate for only one movement, beginning with the body in a specific position, and with an identical goal; and it is probably true that the same response is never made twice when one considers the number of possibilities there are, for example, in shooting a basketball" (Schmidt, 1975, p. 230).

SCHEMA THEORY AND VARIABILITY OF PRACTICE

The importance of highly variable movement experiences is implied from the fact that subjects develop a general memory representation—

Inclusive Basketball, page 124.

a schema—more readily when they are exposed to many variations of an action (Newell, 2003). As previously mentioned, the relationship among four variables during a movement's execution forms the schema, and this relationship is strengthened by the amount and variability of practice. In other words, to perform novel movements successfully in any general class, students should be exposed to a variety of, rather than specific, practice situations during the learning and motor development process. Inclusive basketball on page 124 is a good example of a game that brings some variety to a practice situation.

The schema theory proposes that learners benefit most from executing any primary skill (i.e., kicking, throwing, catching, jumping) in as many different ways and situations and from as many different positions as possible. It confirms a common-sense approach to teaching motor skills to elementary school children: expanding the scope and quality of movement experiences, not confining them to a limited number. Children should not be directed to robotically emulate one "best way" of performing a skill; they are *developing* their best way—certainly, with expert guidance—by approaching each skill in a variety of ways.

Sharon Widmayer, in her article "Schema Theory: An Introduction," states, "Multiple schema-building experiences from multiple perspectives are also needed to help learners develop functional problem-solving schemas that they can use to solve unfamiliar problems (or more accurately, familiar problems in unfamiliar contexts)" (Widmayer, 2007, p. 3).

Variability of practice, therefore, is the key element of the schema theory, which is combined with the philosophy and pedagogy of cooperative learning and brain research in the following chapters.

References

Berthoz, Alain. 2000. *The Brain's Sense of Movement*. Cambridge, MA; London: Harvard University Press.

Brady, Frank. 2004. Children's Organized Sports: A developmental perspective: Despite their place as a childhood rite, youth sports have a high dropout rate. Why? and What can we do about it? *Journal of Physical Education, Recreation & Dance*, Vol. 75.

Erikson, Erik H. 1968. *Identity: Youth and Crisis*. New York: W.W. Norton.

Johnson, David W., Johnson, Roger T., and Holubec, Edythe. The cooperative link. Various Cooperative Learning Institute newsletters, www.co-operation.org.

Newell, Karl M. 2003. Schema theory (1975): Retrospectives and prospectives. *Research Quarterly for Exercise and Sport*. American Alliance for Health, Physical Education, Recreation and Dance, Vol. 74, No. 4, 383-388.

Schmidt, Richard A. 1975, July. A Schema Theory of Discrete Motor Skill Learning." *Psychological Review*, Vol. 82, No. 4.

Schmidt, Richard A. 2003, December. Motor schema theory after 27 years: Reflections and implications for a new theory. *Research Quarterly for Exercise and Sport*, Vol. 74, No. 4, 366-375.

Sherwood, David E., and Lee, Timothy D. 2003. Schema theory: Critical review and implications for the role of cognition in a new theory of motor learning. *Research Quarterly for Exercise and Sport*, Vol. 74, No. 4, 376-382.

Widmayer, Sharon A. 2003. Schema theory: An introduction. Fairfax, VA: George Mason University, Helen A. Keller Institute for Human disabilities, p. 3., www.kihd.gmu.edu/immersion/knowledgebase/strategies/cognitivism/SchemaTheory.htm.

CHAPTER

2

Cooperative Learning

When choosing to focus on cooperation rather than competition to provide students with vigorous physical activity in an enjoyable environment, we should take care not to deny the existence of children's natural tendency to compete. The goal is not to eradicate this mostly healthy human trait, but rather to create conditions in which cooperative behaviors can appear and flourish.

During a recent Balance Week, I decided to use a form of hopscotch game called Jumby from Trinidad and Tobago taken from the book *Games from Long Ago and Far Away*. I told the third-grade students that after completing all seven squares, each player would score a point. The obvious question was immediately fired at me: "Whoever scores the most wins, right?" "No," I said. "You score a point for your group. We'll add all points at the end to see how many points your group scores together." A few minutes later, to my surprise, I saw a boy holding another boy's hand, going through each step of the game, each square, and cheering him on as he overcame his motor difficulties to hopscotch. The conditions for cooperation were favorable.

The 10-year-olds I see, fully padded from head to toe, doing push-ups and being drilled and yelled at when I drive by the fields around Topsfield after school, are the ones who earlier in the day left the gym ecstatic after a full session of a game I call All for One (see chapter 7, page 182). The goal of the game is to keep a beach ball kicked by a fellow student in the air while she completes a short obstacle course and runs back to the base, at which point the whole group receives a point. Groups express their euphoria at surpassing their previous records by a feast of high fives, hugs, jumping, and screaming. I cannot describe the feeling of promoting that sense of community in them.

Some children, even at age 10, benefit from the pressure to triumph like professional athletes. These children have the choice to participate in after-school sports, where such an environment is accepted. In physical education, however, an emphasis on competition and being the strongest, the fastest, or the best offers many children plenty of opportunities for failure.

My intention here is not to engage in philosophical arguments over which is better—competition or cooperation. Such arguments would require an entire book. This book is written for professionals who provide physical activities to groups of children at all levels of physical capabilities and interests, such as in schools. The intention is to present ideas and lesson plans for real classrooms—not ideal ones where all children always compete on an equal footing—while at the same time offering a sound and coherent motor development program.

Cooperative learning relates to the schema theory in that it promotes the use of a variety of movement experiences and a variety of ways to perform any particular skill. In this way, the pressure to emulate the teacher and perform a skill perfectly is lifted from children's shoulders. Motor development becomes an enjoyable experience, not an ordeal of trying to be the best at any given activity.

Physical education classes are ideal situations for a philosophy of teaching such as cooperative learning, in which children are not pitted against one another, classmates are not perceived as obstacles to personal achievement, and active and stimulating physical activity is detached from the internal and external pressure to be the best or to beat others. Children involved in cooperative group activities, such as the game BasketBoom found on page 121, understand that they will not be diminished if a peer performs better. Personal best, caring and sharing, and lighthearted fun permeate the gym environment. Children are given plenty of opportunities for teamwork, communication, coordination, and division of tasks—skills that are necessary throughout life.

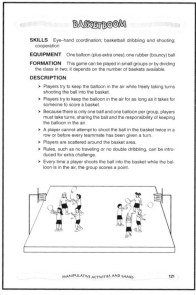

BasketBoom, page 121.

Cooperative learning focuses on children's development rather than on quantitative performance assessment. Children are not evaluated on their physical capabilities, but instead on effort, behavior, and participation.

Following are some games to try with your students that foster cooperative skills:

Johnson, Johnson, and Smith summed up the benefit of cooperative learning as follows:

When engaged in cooperative activities, individuals seek outcomes that are beneficial to themselves *and* to all other members of the group. . . . Cooperation results in participants striving for mutual benefit so that all members of the group benefit from each other's efforts, their recognizing that all group members share a common fate, and that one's performance depends mutually on oneself and one's colleagues (1991, p. 3).

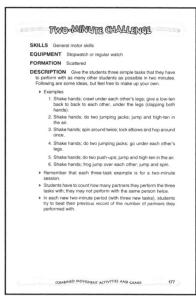

Two-Minute Challenge, page 177.

INGROUPS VERSUS OUTGROUPS

Cooperative learning became a prominent feature of my classes for many reasons, not the least of which were the lack of sad faces exiting the gym, fewer fights, more willingness to participate in gym, and no phone calls from angry parents whose children did not want to attend physical education classes for fear of not being good enough. However, an acquaintance with Henri Tajfel's ideas on social identity theory and Erik Erikson's on group identity compelled me to further explore cooperative learning. Participating in the game or activity, like the Two-Minute Challenge on page 177, becomes the end in itself, thus putting the focus on a sense of fulfillment, instead of on a sense of gratification for winning something or beating others.

"We reflexively divide the human world into ingroups and outgroups. Ingroups are all those categories with which we identify or in which we hold membership, and outgroups are the remaining categories," wrote Bodenhausen (1991, p. 96) about identity and the studies of Tajfel, Erikson, and others. Bodenhausen went on to explain that cooperation is particularly affected by group identification with human subgroups, "even when defined in relatively vague terms as 'fellow university students' or 'people in my experimental group'" (1991, p. 99).

An immediate split into "my group" and "the others" occurs when students are assigned to particular groups distinguished by color, gender, location, or attire. The divide is widened once groups are pitted against one another. Assigning distinctions may unintentionally engender these emotional and psychological feelings of "us vs. them" that favorably regard one's group as compared with the outgroups and is a significant cause of this split.

A positive outcome of team activities is children who normally do not feel that they fully belong to the group, or are not the most sought-after during playtime, suddenly finding themselves completely integrated into a smaller group. To help integrate these students into their groups, one of my rules is that the team with the most scorers, not the one with the most points, wins. I make sure that the activity and the level of skills involved do not promote a premature perception of defeat in the minds of less sports-prone children. I establish the fun character of the activity from the get-go by giving funny names to the teams (cheese puffs, broccoli heads, funky monkeys, crazy chickens). Intergroup handshakes and praise at the end are also a must.

"Things are breaking up. I don't understand why. We began well; we were happy. And then—" says Ralph in William Golding's *Lord of the Flies*, a literary masterpiece on the power of the ingroup and outgroup split. A single physical education class, regrettably, has the potential to emulate the scenario in Golding's story, with children entering the gym as a happy bunch who are excited about the prospect of having a great time together, only to find themselves soon after caught up in angry shouting matches over a point, a play, a turn, or a place. The positive, along with the potentially pernicious, power of group identity should be taken into consideration when working with children.

Activity groups should comprise students with differing social and athletic skills to ensure balance on the teams.

FIVE ELEMENTS OF A COOPERATIVE LESSON

As previously noted, the writings of Johnson, Johnson, and Smith on cooperative learning are invaluable resources to deepen one's understanding of the topic and its application. Other writers who have provided important contributions to the concept of cooperative learning include Robert E. Slavin, Alfie Kohn, and Terry Orlick (who wrote seminal books on cooperative games), and the Brazilian educator Paulo Freire and the Chinese philosopher Confucius.

See table 2.1 on the next page for an introduction to the five elements of a cooperative learning lesson by Johnson, Johnson, and Smith (1991).

As mentioned in table 2.1, a T-chart can be a helpful a tool in building your students' social skills. After choosing a behavior to discuss (e.g., cooperation, respect), students will list what they think that behavior "looks like" in the first column and what that behavior "sounds like" in the second column. This exercise helps students consciously recognize the various ways in which positive reinforcement is communicated (see table 2.2 on page 16).

Table 2.1   Five Basic Elements of a Cooperative Lesson

Positive Interdependence	Students are taught how to work together and depend on each other to achieve success. All students should be given the opportunity to fully participate in group activities, and no one should be rewarded separately from the group—they sink or swim together. As a result, students learn that the abilities of each person in their group are essential for the group's success. See the game Group Balance on page 151.
Face to Face Interaction	Simply stated, face-to-face interaction amounts to "small circles." Students cannot communicate—that is, fully hear or fully listen to each other—when sitting in rows, semicircles, or large squares or when they are allowed to wander around unnecessarily during the processing time (see "Group Processing" in this table). An important feature of active listening is eye contact. Teachers should regularly remind students that spending time in small circles, using "one-foot" voices, and speaking in turn can help a group accomplish its goals.
Individual Accountability	Individual accountability can be assessed by randomly assigning one student from each group to present the group's work and then using that presentation for the entire group's assessment evaluation. Each member may also be graded separately, with the average grade then being applied to each group member. The important thing here is to not assign too much value to final grades. Instead, instill in each student a need to understand the material and, in the case of physical activities, a desire to execute the activity to the best of his or her ability. The focus should be on this process.
Social Skills	Social skills must be taught. The belief that social skills "magically" appear in children without any development is a common misconception. Statements such as "all of you need to cooperate" are vague and ineffective; using practical, clear examples is a better teaching method. Using T-charts modeled on the one following this table can be helpful in teaching students appropriate social skills. Lessons on listening skills, leadership roles, taking turns, etc., should be taught prior to lessons on social skills.
Group Processing	The brain that is doing is the brain that is learning—at least, that's what neurological studies tell us. Allowing students time during and after an activity for self-examination " . . . leads to insight, which in turn leads to increased effectiveness . . . students do not learn from experience they do not reflect on" (Johnson, Johnson, and Smith, 1991).

From D.W. Johnson, R.T. Johnson, and K.A. Smith, "Cooperative Learning: Increasing College Faculty Instructional Productivity," 2001, *ASHE-ERIC Higher Education Research Reports* 20(4): 15-25. Adapted by permission of John Wiley & Sons, Inc.

Table 2.2 Encouraging Positive Reinforcement

Looks like	Sounds like
high five	"nice shot"
thumbs-up	"good throw"
clapping (applause)	"great game"

Reprinted, by permission, from B. Dyson and A. Rubin, 2003, "Implementing Cooperative Learning in Elementary Physical Education," *Journal of Physical Education, Recreation & Dance* 74(1): 49.

COMPETITION

The impulse to succeed appears to be a natural trait of human beings; after all, we would not have overcome tremendous odds and reached our present state of development without this characteristic. Children, for the most part, manifest this natural instinct quite early and quite openly during free play. A few minutes of observing them during recess would discourage anyone from trying to completely eliminate competition from the childhood experience.

Harmful consequences have also resulted from our competitive nature. Left to their own devices, children can easily resort to unsafe actions to satisfy their need to succeed, which can result in negative physical and psychological consequences for themselves and their peers. For this reason, the competitive games and activities throughout this book require more careful planning and oversight than the more cooperative ones do.

A teacher should never allow a child or a team to enter into a competitive situation if the child clearly does not have a shot at winning or accomplishing the task. Competitions such as relay races, dodgeball, and some organized sports can result in a long-lasting negative self-conception and pessimistic perspectives about participation in physical activities in general.

Children generally love to play wheelbarrow, and it is often used as a relay race skill. Instead, I often allow five minutes of free wheelbarrow play in which children naturally decide whether to engage in races. Most children will simply move around, having a great time with their partners.

If you are using competitive activities, such as Extreme Soccer on page 112, make sure that less skilled—or less sports-oriented—children can participate fully and have a fun time using their limited skills. No child should be placed in a situation in which he is expected to perform beyond his skill level.

Other considerations when using competition with elementary school-age children are as follows:

Extreme Soccer, page 112.

> ➢ Deemphasize score keeping.
> ➢ Forbid bragging, teasing, or threatening.
> ➢ Promote students' personal best as opposed to beating opponents. (I expect and constantly remind my children to perform to the best of their abilities, but just as regularly, I assure them that their best is good enough for me and for their team.)
> ➢ Give the activity some measure of fun and humor.
> ➢ Separate best buddies during team sports.
> ➢ Remind students that without the other team there would be no opportunity to enjoy the game. Although they are on opposite sides, they are all partners in fun.

CONCLUSION

To conclude, I offer a quote from "Aidan," a kindergartener, who said in December of the school year: "I was born to be a basketball player, Mr. Dienstmann!"

Aidan began school with severe motor difficulties, not as a result of any diagnosed disability, but instead, due to what I and other colleagues perceive as an extreme case of lack of exposure to physical activities and playtime. His gross motor abilities are still quite poor, and he still needs a lot of practice. However, he feels confident and happy, and he loves to participate in gym.

A program that focused on competition, pitting Aidan's underdeveloped abilities against those of his peers, one that narrowly concentrated on certain sports and their limited number of movement experiences (e.g., kickball), or that required him to perform at a certain ability level to have fun in gym would have certainly aroused feelings of frustration and low self-worth. Instead, he feels good about himself as a physical person, and he is making strides toward becoming an active person. Aidan was a prime candidate to hate physical education classes. Instead, he's been laughing a lot.

Creating a positive experience for all students, including those like Aidan, requires planning and creativity, but it is possible and rewarding. Part II of this book provides some great examples of games and activities that offer inclusive and enjoyable experiences to all students.

In chapter 3, I explain why Aidan's relaxed state of mind and willingness to engage in opportunities for learning are crucial for his success in school. We look at the third topic, brain research on emotions and learning, which combines with the schema theory and cooperative learning to form the pedagogical rationale for *Games for Motor Learning*.

References

Bodenhausen, Galen V. 1991. Identity and cooperative social behavior: Pseudospeciation or human integrations? *World Futures*, Vol. 31, 95-106.

Johnson, D.W., Johnson, R.T, and Smith, K.A. 1991. Cooperative learning: Increasing college faculty instructional productivity. ASHE-ERIC Higher Education Report, No. 4, 3.

Carr, Thomas J., and Deborah C. Wright. *Games from Long Ago and Far Away.* Parker Publishing Company (November 2000) p. 63.

3

Brain Research on Emotions and Learning

Recently, the school where I teach physical education decided to join a fund-raising campaign in which children collect money for a cause while participating in a day of jump rope activities at the school. As I do every year with my early elementary school students, I spent some time introducing the sequence of steps necessary for jumping rope, from having the proper body posture, to simply walking over a jump rope, tossing it overhead, jumping once at a time, all the way to continuous jumping.

Usually, most students master the skills of jumping rope, and the few who don't face the challenge in good spirits and still have fun. This year, however, a few students, unbeknownst to me, became stressed out about their perceived need to be good at jumping rope on the day of the event. Extreme emotional stress resulted in some students' being unable to sleep the night before the event, which, of course, affected their disposition at school the next day. Because I make it a point never to evaluate students at that age on their ability to perform any particular skill, I regretted the whole situation. Needless to say, I was disappointed in myself for not having noticed the emotional escalation.

The obvious point to highlight here is that a simple school assignment or event can have negative effects on the emotional state of students. An unchecked stressful condition can ruin any attempt at teaching or learning.

Emotional states ranging from mild stress to severe distress are constant in the lives of many students. This chapter provides a review of recent research on the effect of emotionally stressful conditions on students' ability to focus, learn, and memorize. An understanding of certain aspects of brain research on emotions can help you choose among the activities presented in the second part of this book.

Equipment Fun, page 74.

The literature on emotions and learning is large and continually growing. In this chapter we explore the following:

➤ *Stress response* is the set of physical manifestations appearing together as a result of stress.

➤ *Fight or flight* is a physical and emotional state preparing the body to face a situation or retreat from it.

➤ *Emotions and learning* are biological occurrences in the brain and how they influence learning.

➤ Several games and activities in part II of this book address the issue of accomplishing motor learning without emotional stress. An example is Equipment Fun from page 74.

STRESS RESPONSE

In his seminal book *The Stress of Life*, Hans Selye (1976), a Canadian endocrinologist, described a set of physiological manifestations appearing together as a result of stress, which is one of bodily or mental tension resulting from factors that tend to alter an existent equilibrium. Selye called this set of manifestations general adaptation syndrome, or GAS. When fully developed, GAS has three stages: the alarm reaction, the stage of resistance, and the stage of exhaustion. Other changes that Selye noted as a result of stress were "loss of body weight, derangement in the regulation of body temperature, disappearance of eosinophil cells from the circulating blood and a number of chemical alterations in the constitution of the body fluids and tissues" (p. 59). (Eosinophils are white blood cells active in allergic diseases, parasitic infections, and other disorders.)

Selye emphasized that stress is not a specific reaction: "The stress response is, by definition, not specific, since it can be produced by virtually any agent. Since stress is the non-specific response of the body to any demand, everybody is always under some degree of stress. Even while quietly asleep our heart must continue to beat, our lungs to breathe, and even our brain works in the form of dreams" (p. 63). He added that stress can only be completely avoided through death.

According to Selye, "It may be said without hesitation that for man the most important stressors are emotional, especially those causing distress"—distress being a harmful variety of stress. Selye further noted that the way stress affects us depends more on how we cope with the stressor than the nature of the stressor itself. Anxiety also causes distress, affecting, for example, test performance. Selye used the example of students who, regardless of their actual success, were praised after an examination and performed better at the following one, contrary to those who were harshly criticized.

Another factor that can hinder performance is the tendency for responses to repeated stress to become exaggerated over time. These responses can become automatic when the same stress factor occurs, even if the situation doesn't warrant such a response. This explains why some students with regular stress in their lives may become overly anxious when faced with minor stresses at school. What a teacher may perceive as a small obstacle may feel like an insurmountable barrier to a student, often with long-lasting effects. By creating a cooperative learning environment (discussed in chapter 2) in physical education classes with games like Togeth'air Ball found on page 126, the unconstructive aspects of stress and the negative emotions that may trigger the stress response syndrome are not present.

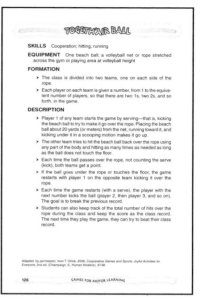

Togeth'air Ball, page 126.

FIGHT OR FLIGHT

Walter Bradford Cannon first coined the phrase *fight or flight response* in the 1920s to describe the animal response to threats (LeDoux, 1996, p. 45). Dr. Neil F. Neimark agrees with Cannon, currently describing this response as "our body's primitive, automatic, inborn response that prepares the body to 'fight' or 'flee' from perceived attack, harm or threat to our survival" (Neimark, n.d., p. 1). In short, the reaction to a threat is instinctual to humans.

The sympathetic nervous system has an active, stimulating function that can cause the heart rate to increase, pupils to dilate, lungs and bronchial tubes to widen for better distribution of oxygen, muscles to tighten, and blood vessels to constrict. An area of the brain called the hypothalamus stimulates the activation of the sympathetic nervous system and the chemical release of certain hormones. One of these hormones, cortisol, sustains the stress response for up to a few hours. However, the prolonged release of stress hormones can damage certain parts of the brain and inhibit some brain functions.

When people perceive danger or are exposed to other stress factors, they become more attentive to the environment than normal as a result of the stimulation of the sympathetic nervous system. This response has helped humans survive. When applied to learning situations, however, this overstimulated state is not favorable. In fact, the fight-or-flight response has been shown to hinder concentration, memorization, and learning.

In the book *Brain Matters: Translating Research Into Classroom Practice*, Patricia Wolfe warned that "a student can perceive even a mild stressor to be threatening, initiating the stress response and lessening the student's ability to perform . . . Under these conditions [being bullied, laughed at, taking part in timed testing, being called on when not prepared, or general fear of failure], emotion is dominant over cognition; and the rational/thinking cortex is less efficient" (Wolfe, 2001, p. 110-111).

Book Action Story, page 169.

Fear—and its resulting release of stress hormones—is removed from the children's experience in class. Fear of underperforming, of not being good at something, of losing, of being humiliated or singled out, or of being seen as unathletic must be eliminated from play. Every physical contribution that each student brings to an activity, such as Book Action Story (found on page 169), is deemed good enough. Focusing on the variability of practice and the richness of experiences over premature fine-tuning and high performance goals can make for a very cooperative class and, by consequence, very low levels of stress.

"When we are under stress, we normally remember less than we otherwise would, and this relates directly to increased cortisol in the system. No wonder it is difficult to focus and remember under stress" (p. 162) wrote Dr. Carla Hannaford, the author of *Smart Moves—Why Learning Is Not All in Your Head* (1995). In support of one of the main arguments of this book, Hannaford concluded this: "Non-competitive, cooperative physical educational programs that encourage student input are fun for everyone. They decrease the stress and, therefore, increase learning power. Taking the unnecessary competition out of our lives will render them less painful and decrease the need for endorphins" (p. 174).

EMOTIONS AND LEARNING

"Human beings have, at best, a very weak control over their emotions; rather, emotions happen to us," wrote neuroscientist Joseph LeDoux (1996). LeDoux clarified that emotions can flood our consciousness "because the wiring of the brain at this point in our evolutionary history is such that connections from the emotional systems to the cognitive systems are stronger than connections from the cognitive systems to the emotional systems" (p. 19). This explains why a constructive, emotionally engaging learning experience facilitates learning.

Because emotions can affect students' behavior below their level of consciousness, they may not be able to explain their feelings. Hence, you need to understand the nature and biology of your students' emotions. Observing students during unstructured time, such as recess, lunch, and after-school activities, can give you insights into the way they actually feel.

Exercises that children associate with positive emotions can help boost self-confidence.

LeDoux explained that the occurrence of any given emotional state motivates future behaviors, again underscoring the importance of positive experiences during the learning process. In physical education, constructive self-images and feelings of self-assurance and confidence in their physical abilities will affect students' future performance.

Animal studies have confirmed what has been observed in humans as well. Among other consequences, stress results in the following:

- Atrophy in brain regions associated with stress
- Cognitive and psychiatric alterations
- Suppression of neurogenesis (the birth of new brain cells)
- Compromised cell survival leading to serious neuronal loss (Sandi, 2004)
- Reduced efficiency of nerve synapses (Oaten and Cheng, 2005)
- Reduced exploratory activity and increased anxiety-like and aggressive behaviors (Oaten and Cheng, 2005)
- Peripheral motion of the eyes and pupil dilation to facilitate scanning the environment for threats (Hannaford, 1995), thus reducing the ability to focus on learning

Mental stress has also been linked to general exhaustion, decreased motivation to learn, and impaired learning performance (LePine, LePine, and Jackson, 2004). College students under the stress of academic examinations, for example, have been found to smoke more and consume more caffeine; have poorer diet habits, emotional control, physical activity, self-care habits, and spending control; and suffer a decline in their sleep and study patterns (Oaten and Cheng, 2005). Needless to say, under such conditions, not much learning can be expected to take place.

Obviously, not every life stressor triggers chains of psychosomatic reactions powerful enough to prevent the normal cognitive functions necessary for learning. Some argue that stress can be divided into challenging and hindrance stresses, in fact, with the former having a positive impact on learning (LePine, LePine, and Jackson, 2004).

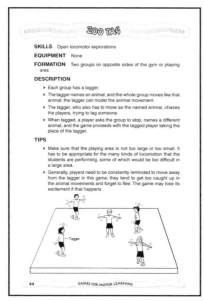

Zoo Tag, page 44.

The authors of "Learned Helplessness Attributional Style and Examination Performance" noted that modest levels of initial failure may be necessary for enhancing future performance in similar tasks (Yee, Pierce, Ptacek, and Modzelesky, 2003). These authors also observed that psychological investment (the perceived importance or relevance of a task to the individual), as opposed to initial failure, may be the deciding factor for future enhanced performance. In other words, tasks in which people have a positive emotional involvement, without stress triggers, are the ones at which they are most likely to excel. Zoo Tag on page 44 is an activity that fosters a psychological investment and arouses specific chemical releases in the brain that create an emotional state most suitable for learning.

Couch Potato Activity, page 168.

Research on the brain indicates that the same pattern of neuronal firing occurs in our brains when we think about an activity as when we are actually doing it. The Couch Potato Activity (page 168) has students imagine the sequence of a skill, which fine-tunes the pattern of neuronal firing before they actually perform the skill.

The following are other great activities found in this book that explore the research on emotions and learning:

In chapter 5—Kicking Feast, page 77; Throwing Feast, page 78; My Favorite Trick, page 79; 10 Ways of Getting the Ball Across, page 80; Throwing Sevens, page 96

In chapter 6—Balance Sculptures, page 140; Crossing Bridges, page 142; Slow Motion Adventures, page 148

As stated, the stress response is associated with the release of cortisol, which sustains the response for up to a few hours, with detrimental effects to cognition. In "Arousal and Cortisol Interact in Modulating Memory Consolidation in Healthy Young Men," Kuhlmann and Wolf (2006) stated that "cortisol enhanced long-term consolidation of emotional stimuli while also impairing consolidation of neutral stimuli" and impairing memory retrieval of emotional stimuli. This can be seen in two ways. One, it shows that students under any kind of perceived or real stress (with the consequent release of cortisol) have a diminished ability to memorize "neutral material"—material devoid of high emotional involvement, which constitutes the majority of content presented to students in school. Two, it demonstrates that the psychological pressure that education generally places on students, as well as constant testing, does not pay off in the end, given that such pressure results in increased levels of cortisol—hindrance stress—and reduced memory retrieval.

Reinforcing this point, Keogh, Bond, and colleagues (2004) described the negative effect that text anxiety brings to performance, even to students who have the skills and cognitive ability to succeed. Anxiety, another aspect of stress, has caused students to be highly distracted by irrelevant thinking, hypersensitive to body sensations, tense, and unable to filter out unrelated material.

One year I had a kindergartener with a diagnosed medical condition that had prevented him from being physically active in his life. Although he was not aware of his condition, his inexperience with active play made him extremely anxious in physical education classes. His eyes were constantly wide open, and I could see his face freezing during my explanations of the days' activities. As a result of his stressed mental state, his movements were noticeably stiff. He would run as though his knee joints were locked. For a few months, I got on my knees to listen and talk to him at eye level, listened to his every concern and assured him that he could rest whenever he wanted, modified activities according to his perceived capabilities, and most important, explained that he would not be forced into anything. Four months later I heard from his parents that he got up one morning excited about having gym that day. Two weeks later he caught up with the rest of the class during a fun running game.

Finally, Kaikh, Kahloon, and colleagues (2004) asserted that exercise is said to be one of three or four primary factors for regulating and counteracting the harmful effects of stress, which seems to be increasing, or at least not subsiding, in modern society. At an early age, students should be given ample opportunities to be physically active and should be informed of the many benefits of exercise—recreational or competitive. Thus, it seems to be highly counterproductive to the mental and physical health of students to reduce the frequency and importance of physical education in their lives, as seems to be the case in many school districts across the United States and in other countries in recent years.

EXPLAINING THE MAIN IDEA

The merging of the three elements that form this book—the schema theory of discrete motor skill learning, cooperative learning, and brain research on emotions and learning—is summarized in the following statement, also presented at the start of chapter 1:

> Highly variable movement experiences encourage cooperative learning. The resulting low mental stress enhances learning, enjoyment, and long-term retention of learned skills, according to current research on the brain.

It is time to further elaborate on this statement. Varying the ways to perform a skill during the learning process keeps students from having to concentrate too soon on refining it. Movement learning should naturally develop from universal to complex, gradually progressing from general to specific. Children should be encouraged to experiment. You can still give them suggestions and ideas, but more important, give them plenty of opportunities to explore the possibilities that the task at hand (or the equipment being used) offers. Of course, always observe safe practices when offering a variety of experiences.

By replacing competitive goals with the concept of students' personal best, you remove a substantial amount of mental pressure and peer pressure from the learning environment. After being consistently exposed to such lessons, the children internalize this concept. The pursuit of students' personal best and lighthearted fun generally result.

Games that reflect the concepts of schema theory, cooperative learning, and stress reduction are outlined in part II.

References

Hannaford, Carla. 1995. *Smart moves—Why learning is not all in your head.* Arlington, VA: Great Ocean.

Kaikh, Babar T., Kahloon, Arsalan, et al. 2004, November. Students, stress and coping strategies: A case of Pakistani Medical School. *Education for Health*, Vol. 17, No. 3, 346-353.

Keogh, Edmund, Bond, Frank W., et al. 2004, September. Test anxiety, susceptibility to distraction and examination performance. *Anxiety, Stress, and Coping*, Vol. 17, No. 3, 241-252.

Kuhlmann, Sabrina, and Wolf, Oliver T. 2006. Arousal and cortisol interact in modulating memory consolidation in healthy young men. *Behavioral Neuroscience*, Vol. 120, No. 1, 217-223.

LeDoux, Joseph. 1996. *The emotional brain—The mysterious underpinnings of emotional life.* New York: Simon & Schuster.

LePine, Jeffrey A., LePine, Marcie A., and Jackson, Christine L. 2004. Challenge and hindrance stress: Relationships with exhaustion, motivation to learn, and learning performance. *Journal of Applied Psychology*, Vol. 89, No. 5, 883-891.

Neimark, Neil F. n.d. The fight or flight response. Mind/Body Education Center, www.thebodysoulconnection.com.

Oaten, Megan, and Cheng, Ken. 2005. Academic examination stress impairs self-control. *Journal of Social and Clinical Psychology*, Vol. 24, No. 2, 254-279.

Sandi, Carmen. 2004, December. Stress, cognitive impairment and cell adhesion molecules. *Nature Reviews*, Neuroscience, Vol. 5.

Selye, Hans. 1976. *The stress of life*, rev. ed. New York: McGraw-Hill.

Wolfe, Patricia. 2001 *Brain matters: Translating research into classroom practice*. Alexndria, VA: Association for Supervision and Curriculum Development.

Yee, Penny L., Pierce, Gregory R., Ptacek, J.T., and Modzelesky, Kristine L. 2003, December. Learned helplessness attributional style and examination performance: Enhancement effects are not necessarily moderated by prior failure. *Anxiety, Stress and Coping,* Vol. 16, No. 4, 359-373.

MOTOR DEVELOPMENT GAMES AND ACTIVITIES

4

Locomotor Activities and Games

This chapter offers activities and games that help children explore and perfect the many ways in which they move their bodies from place to place, including walking, speed walking, running, jumping, hopping, skipping, and crawling. Most of the activities in the remaining chapters comply with the schema theory in terms of offering many variations of the skills (e.g., Marshmallow Hike on page 34). Other games make use of these skills through very active, fun, and inclusive workouts. Either way, it's important to introduce any activity to the students by presenting a global idea first. For example, "We are going to play a toss and catch game," or "The next game will be a running and tagging game." The point is to proceed from larger to finer details. When it is possible, I skip one or two minor rules of the game until the first rest break to give students time to process the overall idea.

Children will have a great, sweaty, fun time with the 100-plus activities that follow!

ROCK AND TALK

SKILLS Various locomotor and social skills

EQUIPMENT Fun music

FORMATION Free

DESCRIPTION This can be the first locomotor activity of the year. It's fun, it has plenty of movement variations and resting stops, and students can get to know a bit more about their new classmates.

> Give students a locomotor movement, such as running, skipping, galloping, sliding, crab walking, frog jumping, speed walking, slow-motion running, dancing funny, walking funny, leaping, mummy walking, or air swimming, and explain that they are to do this movement while the music is playing. Start the music.

> When the music stops—after 20 to 30 seconds—each student quickly looks for the closest available partner.

> Partners quietly shake hands and listen to your directions. Give them a discussion topic (see examples at the end of these directions).

> After 10 to 15 seconds of discussion, give the students the next locomotor command and say, "Go."

> Each time the music stops, the students have to shake hands with a different partner. They may never turn their backs to someone coming to shake their hands. Explain the necessary social skills for this activity before beginning.

> Here are examples of Rock and Talk discussion topics:

    1. Your full name and where you were born

    2. The best thing you did over the summer

    3. Your parents' full names and their professions

    4. Your favorite thing to do after school

    5. Your favorite book

    6. What you'd like to do when you grow up

    7. Your favorite place to go

    8. Your favorite thing to do at recess

    9. Your most memorable day at school

SAFE INDOOR RUNNING

SKILLS   Running safely among others; spatial awareness

EQUIPMENT   None

FORMATION   Scattered

DESCRIPTION   This is also an activity that should be introduced at the beginning of the year. After witnessing so many crashes and body slamming in the gym, I devised this activity to instill in students a sense of when it is appropriate and safe to run fast among other players, and when they should use extra care.

> ➤ Ask students to walk around the gym or playing area looking for personal spaces (spots with fewer players).

> ➤ When they find an open space, they speed walk; when approaching someone or being approached, they must slow down.

> ➤ The more people they find around them, the slower they must walk; the fewer people, the faster they can walk.

> ➤ Enforce the rules! This activity works best when done quietly; explain the importance of this skill for future enjoyment of gym classes.

> ➤ Repeat this activity using half the gym or playing area only.

> ➤ Begin the activity again, this time using jogging or running first with the full gym or playing area and then half of it.

> ➤ Repeat this activity a few times at the beginning of the year; it should last about five minutes.

MARSHMALLOW HIKE

SKILL   Walking variability

EQUIPMENT   None

FORMATION   Scattered

DESCRIPTION   This activity exemplifies the use of high variability of practice within the skill of walking.

> By imagining a variety of surfaces to walk on, students naturally explore various ways of walking and use muscles in distinct ways, which improve balance.

> List many types of real or unreal walking surfaces and challenge the students to demonstrate how it would look to walk over them.

> Examples: walk over marshmallows, on tacks, in deep water, on hot sand, in bubble gum, in mud, on wet grass, in quicksand, in peanut butter, on feathers, on bouncy rubber, on marbles, on a thick carpet, on ice, over big rocks, on cockroaches, in wet cement, in snow, on the moon.

> Always give students the chance to make suggestions in activities of this sort. End this activity with students' suggestions.

10 WAYS TO CROSS

SKILLS   Open exploration of locomotor skills

EQUIPMENT   None

FORMATION   Students stand at one end of the gym or playing area, side by side.

DESCRIPTION   This is a locomotor activity exploring creativity and variability of movement.

> Students stand side by side at one end of the gym or playing area.

> Instruct students to cross the area 10 times, performing a different locomotor movement each time. Tell them they should not simply walk and that they can borrow ideas from their peers.

> Praise students who come up with challenging ideas.

> Remind them to keep track of the number of crossings and never repeat the same movement twice.

VARIATION   Have students do the same activity but in pairs. This is a favorite of my students.

WANT A BUS RIDE?

SKILLS Open exploration of locomotor skills

EQUIPMENT Small and large hula hoops

FORMATION A few hoops on the ground; about four students with hoops around their hips wandering freely around the gym

DESCRIPTION This activity was invented by some of my students. The beauty of it rests in its simplicity and the genuine fun they have playing it.

> ➤ Hoops on the ground are bus stations where students are waiting for the bus.

> ➤ Students with small hoops around their waists move around the area picking up students (they can take only one at a time) and dropping them at other stations.

> ➤ Students at the stations wait for the bus to pass by their station and hook up behind the driver by holding on to the hoop and going in tandem to another station.

> ➤ Students can choose how long they want to travel and at which station to get off.

> ➤ This game can be played using many forms of locomotion.

> ➤ Choose new bus drivers after a while.

Bus driver

Bus station (hula hoop on floor)

MY HAPPY FEET

SKILLS   Leg and foot agility

EQUIPMENT   Music

FORMATION   Scattered

DESCRIPTION   This activity can be a good introduction to foot and leg agility.

> Play some fun music.
> Ask students to dance while following your instructions: giant steps, moving feet very fast, slow motion, touching only the gym lines, not touching the lines but moving over them, dancing only on their heels, dancing only on their toes, tap dancing with the rhythm of the song, dancing funny, and so forth.

SPINNING STARS

SKILLS Cooperation; locomotor exploration

EQUIPMENT None

FORMATION Four students holding hands in a cross shape at the center (their left hands are all touching); the remaining students are lined up a few yards (or meters) away.

DESCRIPTION

> ➤ The students holding hands begin to walk slowly counterclockwise with their right hands extended to form a spinning star. Send the remaining students, lined up away from the star, one by one to join one of the points of the star by taking the hand of one of the students.

> ➤ As more players are sent in, tell the spinning star to move slightly faster (speed walking is recommended) until the star breaks down and everyone gets a big laugh.

> ➤ Begin the star again with new students moving clockwise. Students can also try skipping.

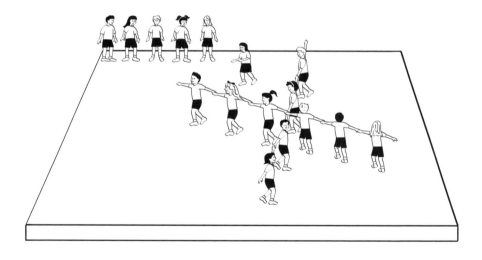

GUIDE AND TRAVELER

SKILLS   Any locomotor movement; open movement exploration

EQUIPMENT   None

FORMATION   Groups of two or three

DESCRIPTION

> ➤ Have each group decide which member starts as the travel guide.

> ➤ The guide makes up an imaginary trip for the travelers, explaining where they are (such as crossing a river or going through a forest, a city, outer space, the ocean, a scary tunnel) and what they are going to do there (ride an airplane, ride horses, ride bicycles, board a ship, wrestle gorillas, fly like eagles).

> ➤ After the guide explains the trip, the group performs the task together.

> ➤ After about three minutes the groups choose another guide and begin another trip.

TIP   This activity encourages creativity, free exploration, imagination, and organizing skills. Explain to students that they are to think of exciting things to do that are safe for all students (no dangerous or complicated gymnastics movements).

CRAZY TRAINS

SKILLS   Various locomotor movements

EQUIPMENT   None

FORMATION   Groups of four to six students

DESCRIPTION

> Students stand in line, forming a little train, connected to each other in any way they want.

> The train can move in many ways. Students think of several fun, funny, interesting, challenging ways that their train can move: forward, backward, sideways, zigzag, dancing, skipping, crawling, walking funny.

> With every new locomotor idea, a new student becomes the conductor, who is the first person in the line.

Crazy Trains is a great activity in which to use fun, jumpy music. Whenever appropriate, I try to play groovy tunes. Lively music always increases the excitement level and helps the students internalize the perception of the gym as a place where they will have a great time. Play music often.

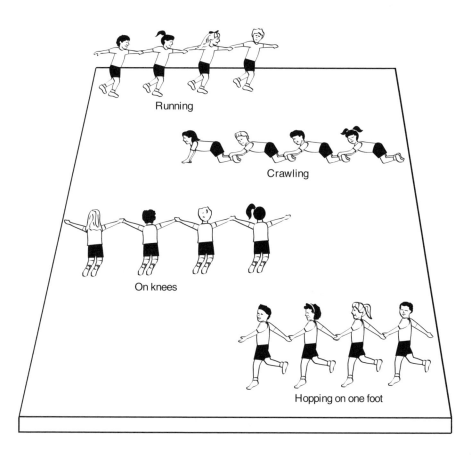

Running

Crawling

On knees

Hopping on one foot

WILD HORSES

SKILL Galloping

EQUIPMENT Long foam noodles

FORMATION Groups of three mounted on a single noodle; three or four students are lone riders

DESCRIPTION This is a great game to play after introducing children to galloping skills. Be prepared for uproarious laughter.

> ➤ A group of three players mounts the noodle and gallops together as though on a horse.
> ➤ A small end of the noodle should be left behind the last player.
> ➤ The group is galloping away from the lone riders, who try to climb on the backs of the horses.
> ➤ If successful, the lone rider yells to the front rider, "Lone rider Marc (or Mary)," and the player named becomes the new lone rider and has to chase other horses (galloping) to climb on.
> ➤ Watch for safe speed. Front riders should not change direction too suddenly because it may throw the others off.

Galloping on noodle

Lone rider

THE BUG GAME

SKILLS   Open locomotor explorations

EQUIPMENT   None

FORMATION   Scattered

DESCRIPTION

> ➤ Each student chooses a kind of bug and begins to act like it.

> ➤ Students go around the gym or playing area silently looking for others that they think might be the same bug as they are, judging only by the way they are acting.

> ➤ Once they believe they have found the same bug as they are, students stay with that bug and go around looking for more bugs like them.

> ➤ Students who do not find more bugs like them can choose another bug to be and start the search over.

ZOO TAG

SKILLS Open locomotor explorations

EQUIPMENT None

FORMATION Two groups on opposite sides of the gym or playing area

DESCRIPTION

> Each group has a tagger.
> The tagger names an animal, and the whole group moves like that animal; the tagger can model the animal movement.
> The tagger, who also has to move as the named animal, chases the players, trying to tag someone.
> When tagged, a player asks the group to stop, names a different animal, and the game proceeds with the tagged player taking the place of the tagger.

TIPS

> Make sure that the playing area is not too large or too small. It has to be appropriate for the many kinds of locomotion that the students are performing, some of which would be too difficult in a large area.
> Generally, players need to be constantly reminded to move away from the tagger in this game; they tend to get too caught up in the animal movements and forget to flee. The game may lose its excitement if that happens.

RUNNING FEAST

SKILL   Variations on running

EQUIPMENT   None

FORMATION   Scattered

DESCRIPTION   This is a great warm-up and a great way to introduce the idea that any skill may be explored in infinite ways to increase general agility.

> ➤ Explain the many ways of running.
> ➤ Allow students to make suggestions.
> ➤ Examples: running funny, with various body shapes, with hands on the head, with arms crossed, dragging fingers along the floor, holding knees, holding toes, holding ankles, with knees "glued," kicking buttocks with ankles, very tall, very small, crossing legs, with one foot on tiptoe, on one heel.

MISSION TO MARS

SKILLS   Various locomotor movements; open movement exploration

EQUIPMENT   None

FORMATION   Scattered

DESCRIPTION   This activity works as a lively warm-up. A series of commands takes students through an imaginary trip to Mars:

> ➤ Warm up the engine—short, squatting jumps.
> ➤ Lift off—hands over the head in a rocket position; jump off
> ➤ Slowly take off—running, speeding up slowly.
> ➤ Dodge asteroids—flying in space, dodging asteroids.
> ➤ Move in space—slow-motion movements.
> ➤ Spin out of control—spinning, swirling.
> ➤ Fly smoothly.
> ➤ Circle around Mars—circling fast to slow.
> ➤ Land on Mars.
> ➤ Become Martians—acting out ideas of Martians.
> ➤ Lift off from Mars—end. Start again, this time scrambling the commands.

JUMPING LAND

SKILL   Jumping

EQUIPMENT   None

FORMATION   Scattered

DESCRIPTION   Children love to jump. A lesson on many ways of jumping can be extremely fun, as well as helping to strengthen the fundamental skill of jumping.

> ➤ You can direct this activity, giving students all kinds of jumping ideas, or, preferably, you could have the students scatter around the playing area and ask them for suggestions on jumping.

> ➤ The group follows a student's idea after he demonstrates—until you pick a new student.

> ➤ Some examples: jumping in various directions (make sure they look behind them before jumping backward), a certain distance, in place at various speeds, while turning in the air, while moving legs in the air, with crossed legs, while kicking one foot forward or backward, as high as possible (students should tell how they accomplish a high jump), while reaching up, creatively with a partner, landing lightly, landing heavily.

MUTATIONS

SKILLS   Any locomotor movement; open movement exploration

EQUIPMENT   None

FORMATION   Scattered

DESCRIPTION   Anyone who works with children knows how much they love to imitate. Physical education classes give them the opportunity to mutate into all imaginable roles. In this lesson they explore several locomotor movements by becoming different people, objects, and so forth. This is also a great lesson on body awareness. Here are some suggestions:

> People—firefighter, airplane pilot, mountain climber, cowboy or cowgirl, builder

> Story characters—witch, giant, dragon, monster, knight

> Objects—swing, yo-yo, ball, stapler

> Weather conditions—wind, hurricane, lightning, blizzard

> Machines—soda machine, rocket, bulldozer, canoe, seesaw, helicopter, vacuum cleaner, garbage truck, popcorn machine

> Animals—hummingbird, vultures, kangaroo, chicken, caterpillar, seal

SNAKES, RATS, AND ROBOTS

SKILLS   Crawling; slithering; speed walking

EQUIPMENT   Beanbags, cones, hula hoops

FORMATION

> ➤ Divide the class into three groups.
> ➤ Choose two students to be snakes and two to be robots; the remaining students in the group are rats.
> ➤ Set up each group in an area that is circled by cones with the beanbags in the center (put the beanbags inside a hula hoop).

DESCRIPTION   I spend a lot of time thinking up games in which students can practice certain motor skills in a fun way, taking away the perception of drilling or dull repetitions. This game is one example of trying to achieve this goal.

> ➤ The snakes stay within the cones' boundaries, moving like snakes, protecting the treasure (the beanbags), and trying to tag other teams' robots who enter the area (the safe) to steal beanbags one at a time. When a robot gets tagged by a snake, the robot has to go back to its area.
> ➤ Snakes have to be on their bellies at all times.
> ➤ Rats crawl around the gym trying to tag robots before they can reach the safe. When a rat tags a robot, the robot also goes back to its original area before attempting to go out to steal beanbags again.
> ➤ Robots do not tag anyone; they are the only ones who can steal the treasure from other teams, one beanbag at a time.
> ➤ Robots must speed walk only and cannot jump over snakes to steal the treasure.
> ➤ Robots who get tagged inside the safe when stealing a beanbag have to return the beanbag and go back to their areas.
> ➤ After stealing a beanbag and exiting an opponent's safe, a robot cannot be tagged anymore, until it has deposited the beanbag in its own safe.
> ➤ The game ends when one team does not have any more beanbags. Players then switch their roles and the game restarts.

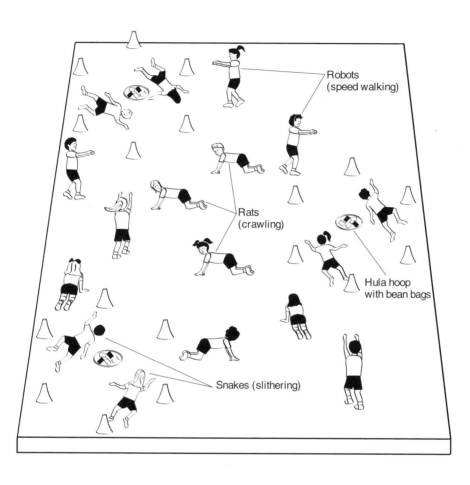

Robots
(speed walking)

Rats
(crawling)

Hula hoop
with bean bags

Snakes (slithering)

HIGH TENS

SKILLS Running; crawling

EQUIPMENT Four pinnies

FORMATION Four or five taggers; the remaining players are scattered

DESCRIPTION

> Choose four players to be taggers and have them wear pinnies.

> Taggers chase the players, who, when tagged, have to freeze standing up with arms crossed and legs spread apart.

> Players can save frozen (tagged) players by performing the following three steps:

1. Shake hands.

2. Crawl under the frozen players' legs in a figure eight.

3. Both players jump and clap both hands in the air (a high ten).

> Taggers may not tag players while they are performing the preceding steps, and they cannot stand babysitting next to them to catch them as they run.

> After a few minutes, pick new taggers.

Crawling under legs

Frozen player

Chasing

Giving a high ten

Handshake

FARMERS AND CHICKENS

SKILL   Running

EQUIPMENT   Several tennis balls; six cones

FORMATION   About a third of the students are farmers (they are taggers); the rest are chickens.

DESCRIPTION

> ➤ This is a tag game. Farmers are taggers. Chickens start the game with two eggs (tennis balls), one in each hand.

> ➤ Farmers want to steal the eggs from the chickens by tagging the chickens on their hands or on the tennis balls they are holding.

> ➤ A chicken who is tagged gives both eggs to the farmer, at which point they switch roles; the farmer—who is now holding one egg in each hand—becomes a chicken. No tag-backs.

> ➤ Chickens can go to an area—a circle of cones, for example—to lay eggs (while sitting and acting like chickens) and rest for about 10 seconds, whenever needed (but not too often).

TIPS

> ➤ Farmers are not to grab chickens in an attempt to tag.

> ➤ Chickens cannot hide the eggs behind their backs or under their arms, pretending that they do not have them—it confuses every-one.

TAG THEM ALL

SKILLS Speed walking; crawling

EQUIPMENT None

FORMATION Scattered

DESCRIPTION The object of this game is to crawl under the legs of the most playmates as possible in two minutes.

> On "Go," all players begin to speed walk trying to tag each other.
> When tagged, a player freezes, standing up, with legs apart to allow the tagger to crawl underneath.
> After completing this task, players continue playing as before.
> Players cannot tag the same person twice.
> Players may not immediately tag players who are finishing crawling under their legs. They have to be speed walking to be tagged.
> Have students play this game twice or more to allow them to improve their records.

MOSQUITOES, BEARS, AND SALMON

SKILLS   Running; visual and motor reaction

EQUIPMENT   Two rows of cones, or lines on the floor

FORMATION   Two groups on opposite sides of the playing area

DESCRIPTION   This game is similar to Rock, Paper, Scissors: bear beats salmon, salmon beats mosquito, and mosquito beats bear (believe it or not!).

> ➤ Each group huddles and quietly chooses one of the three options: mosquitoes, bears, or salmon. The other group must not hear their choice.

> ➤ Both groups then meet in the center, where they line up facing each other. On the count of three, each group demonstrates their choice: salmon make fish faces and swerving motions with their hands; mosquitoes spread their arms and shake their hands, making buzzing noises; and bears raise their arms and growl ferociously.

> ➤ The winning team chases the other.

> ➤ Players tagged before they can cross the line of cones at the end of the playing area have to join the other team.

> ➤ Restart the game.

> ➤ In case of a tie during the face-off, players go back, huddle, and play again.

TIPS

> ➤ Players should be quiet when huddling.

> ➤ Everyone needs to be included in the huddle.

> ➤ Players should go together as a group to the middle to face the other team.

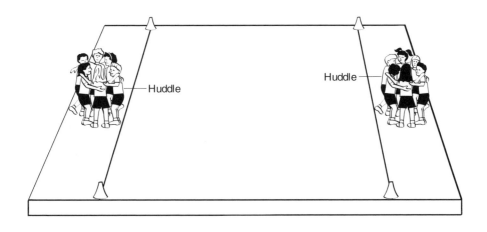

Huddle

Huddle

Face-off = Mosquitoes beat bears

Bears   Mosquitoes

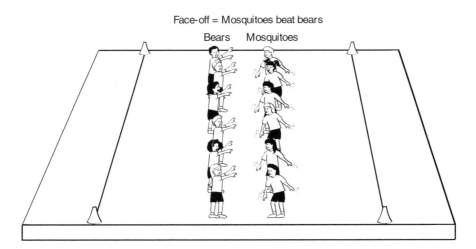

LINE TAG

SKILL Running

EQUIPMENT Two balls

FORMATION

> Two taggers, each with one ball, run on lines on the floor.

> The remaining players also run on the lines.

DESCRIPTION

> Taggers run after the players trying to touch (tag) them with the ball; once tagged, the player takes the ball and becomes the new tagger.

> All players and taggers have to stay on the lines.

> The most important rule of the game is that no one is allowed to pass another player.

> When two players run into each other from opposite directions, one of them has to turn around. Players decide who turns around based on the positions of the taggers.

> If a player is being chased by a tagger and several players are blocking the way, all the players in the way must turn around and run the other way.

> Rules should be strictly enforced so the game is fair for everyone.

TIP When teaching this game to younger children, you can have them simply run around the gym or playing area, staying on the lines and never passing each other. This gives them a chance to practice the concept of not passing and also introduces the central focus of this game, which is to develop cooperative strategies to escape from taggers.

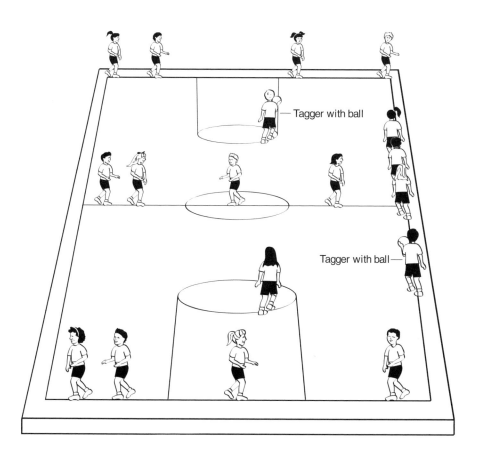

Tagger with ball

Tagger with ball—

KING CAESAR (QUEEN ITALY)

SKILLS   Running; foot agility

EQUIPMENT   12 cones

FORMATION

> Chose one student to start as the king or queen. That student goes to the middle of the playing field.

> All other students go inside the three castles (formed by four cones set in a square). Set castles far enough from each other to provide a challenging running area between them.

DESCRIPTION   This game is fabulous. I have modified it from another book and have been teaching it in schools and summer camps for years. It is always a tremendous hit. It's more complicated than the average game, but it's worth the time spent understanding it. Basically, the game is divided into two parts:

PART I

1. The King Caesar (Queen Italy) begins the game in the middle of the area.
2. Players are safe as long as they are in a castle. They may leave one castle to go to another whenever they feel they can make it there safely.
3. Captured slaves (tagged players) chase the remaining players and help capture them for the king or queen. (The king or queen plus the slaves are all running freely through the playing area, though they can't invade a castle.)
4. The king or queen has two jobs: to capture slaves by tagging players running from castle to castle and to be on the lookout for empty castles to take over.
5. When the king or queen invades an empty castle, he or she yells "king's castle" or "queen's castle" and all players must freeze.

PART II

1. The king or queen steps out of the invaded castle and picks one of the frozen players, who now tries to enter the king's or queen's castle without getting tagged.
2. The king or queen protects the castle (but cannot be inside in this one-on-one challenge), trying to tag the chosen player.

3. If the chosen player enters the castle without being tagged, that player becomes the new king or queen.

4. If tagged before being able to enter the king's or queen's castle, the chosen player goes back to the spot where she was frozen, and the king or queen challenges another player to try to enter the castle.

5. If too many players are unsuccessful in their attempts to enter the king's or queen's castle, the king or queen simply names another player to be the next king or queen and the game restarts from the beginning.

TIPS

➤ No sliding into the castles; it is too dangerous. Runners coming from different directions can get hurt.

➤ When a king or queen takes over a castle, players must immediately freeze; they may not continue moving toward the king or queen in the hope of being chosen to invade.

➤ Enforcing the rules guarantees success and fun.

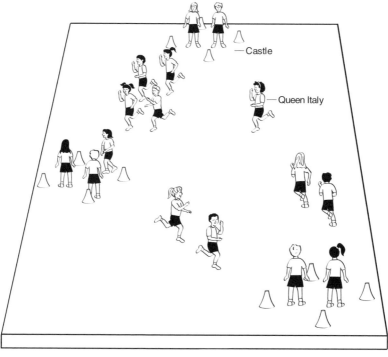

SNAKE HUNTERS

SKILLS Running; foot agility

EQUIPMENT Jump ropes

FORMATION A third of the students are snake hunters; the remaining students are snakes and receive jump ropes.

DESCRIPTION

> ➤ Direct snakes to jog or run, holding their jump ropes behind them while shaking them on the floor.
> ➤ A hunter captures a snake by stepping on the rope. At that point, the hunter and snake switch roles.

TIPS

> ➤ Students should shake jump ropes close to the ground to prevent injury.
> ➤ When running with a rope, students need to keep their heads up and look forward to prevent collisions.
> ➤ Students should hold ropes lightly and behind them (like tails), so they slip off their hands easily once stepped on.
> ➤ Snakes cannot fight for their ropes once they have been stepped on. They must let them go easily and go after another player. No tag-backs.

TURTLES AND EAGLES

SKILL   Running

EQUIPMENT   Old towels and pinnies

FORMATION   Three students are eagles (taggers), two are savers (each with a towel), and the rest are turtles.

DESCRIPTION

> Eagles chase the turtles and try to tag them.

> When tagged, a turtle freezes on the ground in a turtle position (tucked in with the face between the knees).

> A player is saved when one of the savers covers her with the towel to hide her from the eagles flying overhead.

> The turtle that has been saved keeps the towel and goes around the playing field looking for another player to save.

> Choose new eagles every few minutes.

> Savers carrying towels cannot be tagged by eagles.

> If a tagged player is not in a turtle position, he cannot be saved.

CHICKEN SHACK TAG

SKILLS   Running; dodging; foot agility

EQUIPMENT   Five rubber chickens; cones; pinnies; foam balls

FORMATION

> ➤ Five chicken taggers wear pinnies, and each carries a rubber chicken.
> ➤ All the other players are chickens.
> ➤ Set up a small circle of cones (the chicken shack) in the middle of the playing field.
> ➤ Place the foam balls (eggs) inside the chicken shack.
> ➤ Two chicken taggers guard the chicken shack by running around it and protecting the eggs from being stolen. The other three chicken taggers run after the chickens trying to tag them. The guarding and running chicken taggers should switch places after a couple of minutes.

DESCRIPTION   This is another crown jewel of a game. Because it is somewhat complicated, you will need a little extra time explaining it at the beginning. Children cannot stop playing once they get it!

> ➤ At the start, the game looks as follows: Eggs are all in the shack; two taggers protect the shack; three taggers are running around after the chickens; chickens are escaping from taggers and at the same time trying to go into the shack to steal one egg at a time.
> ➤ Tagged chickens must go into the chicken shack to lay eggs (sit over a ball).
> ➤ Other chickens may save the ones laying eggs by going into the shack and lightly touching their heads. Taggers may tag the chickens trying to save the ones laying eggs.
> ➤ The saved chicken gets a free walk out of the shack. A chicken cannot be tagged leaving the shack, nor can he immediately turn to grab an egg.
> ➤ Chickens may also try to go into the chicken shack and steal one egg, after which they may run around holding the egg; if tagged, they do not need to go into the chicken shack. Rather, they must put the egg back in the shack and can continue playing. (They get a free walk out after returning an egg to the chicken shack.)

- ➤ Chickens can have only one egg at a time.
- ➤ Chickens can go into the shack and do two things simultaneously: steal one egg and save another chicken, but if tagged in this process, they have to sit down and lay eggs as well.
- ➤ After a few minutes, choose five new taggers.

Taggers

Laying eggs

ALIENS AND HUMANS

SKILLS   Running; hand dexterity

EQUIPMENT   Several flags or small scarves

FORMATION   Five taggers (aliens); the remaining players are humans and receive flags.

DESCRIPTION

> ➤ The game begins with five alien taggers (players without flags).

> ➤ The remaining players, humans, wear flags tucked into the sides of their pants or shorts, not the front or back; flags should be hanging down and showing clearly.

> ➤ To become humans, the aliens need to steal a flag, after which they may go to a predetermined area—the alien mutation chamber—to safely tuck in the flag and come back to the game as a human.

> ➤ The player who lost the flag is the new alien and runs after other humans. She cannot steal the flag from the same person who stole hers.

> ➤ Because this is a very fast-paced game, breaks might be necessary.

TIPS

> ➤ Humans may not hold on to their flags when chased by aliens.

> ➤ Aliens may not push, trip, or grab humans in an effort to steal their flags.

> ➤ If a human drops a flag while running, aliens are allowed to pick it up and become humans.

VARIATION   To add some manipulative challenge, give each player a playground ball to dribble as they play the game.

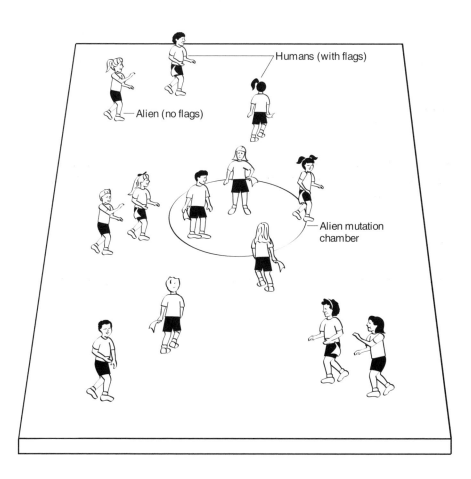

Humans (with flags)

Alien (no flags)

Alien mutation chamber

AMOEBA TAG

SKILLS   Running; foot and hand agility

EQUIPMENT   None

FORMATION   Groups of four players are ideal; no group should have more than five players.

DESCRIPTION

> ➤ Four players to a group; one is the tagger.
> ➤ The three remaining players hold hands in a circle, forming an amoeba.
> ➤ Standing a few feet from the amoeba, the tagger names one person in the group to try to tag.
> ➤ The tagger runs around the group trying to tag the chosen player. The other players protect that player by keeping their bodies between the tagger and the chosen person—while always holding hands.
> ➤ The amoeba moves in a circle, with the tagger circling around.
> ➤ Once the chosen player is tagged, the tagger and the tagged player switch places.

TIPS

> ➤ The tagger cannot go through the middle, sticking a hand across to tag the chosen player; he must work around the outside of the group.
> ➤ The group works together to keep the tagger from tagging the chosen member.
> ➤ The amoeba should try not to travel far from the original area.

POP-UP TAG

SKILLS Running; hand agility

EQUIPMENT None

FORMATION Scattered; everyone is a tagger simultaneously.

DESCRIPTION I do not know who made up this game, but your students will love it.

> ➤ On "Go," any player can tag another player.
> ➤ When tagged, a player sits down and has to remain seated until the one who tagged her gets tagged. At that point she can get up and play again.
> ➤ Remind students to keep watching the player who tagged them, so they know when to get up again.
> ➤ In this game, players often tag each other at the same time. When this happens, they play Rock, Paper, Scissors to decide who has to sit.

TIP If someone is tagged just before tagging another player, there's no need for Rock, Paper, Scissors. Students should be expected to be fair.

VARIATION Every player has a soft foam Frisbee and tries to tag others by tossing the Frisbee at them. A player is tagged only if the Frisbee touches him anywhere from the neck down.

10-SECOND TAG

SKILLS   Running; tagging; dodging

EQUIPMENT   Stopwatch

FORMATION   Three players stand out of the running area; the remaining players scatter around.

DESCRIPTION

> ➤ Select three students to start at the taggers' line, the sideline next to where you are standing.
> ➤ On "Go," the first person in the taggers' line has 10 seconds to tag as many players as he can.
> ➤ Once 10 seconds are up, blow a whistle. The tagger may stay in the playing area if he has tagged someone.
> ➤ Set up a square of cones in one corner of the playing area to serve as an exercise area.
> ➤ All those who are tagged go to the exercise area to perform a couple of preestablished exercises.
> ➤ Once a player has finished the exercises, she goes to the end of the taggers' line to wait for her turn to become a tagger.
> ➤ If the tagger does not tag anyone in 10 seconds, he then has to go to the exercise area to perform the exercises, and then go back to the end of the taggers' line.
> ➤ In other words, every 10 seconds a new tagger is sent in and the previous one leaves (if she didn't tag anyone) or stays (if she tagged someone).

TIPS

> ➤ Send only one tagger at a time.
> ➤ The exercise area should be set away from the playing/running area.
> ➤ When chased or chasing, players may not run inside the exercise square or behind the taggers' line.

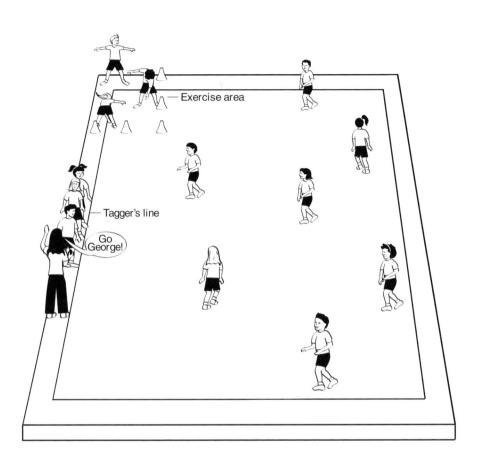

CHAPTER

5

Manipulative Activities and Games

The first activity in this chapter, Combined Approach to Teaching a Skill, illustrates an approach to teaching the skills necessary for participating in games and activities. You may use it as a framework for putting the schema theory (see chapter 1) into practice with your students. This is followed by activities and games that allow children to explore and develop a relationship with each piece of equipment before being asked to use it to perform specific techniques (see Equipment Exploration on page 76). The following games include the elements of cooperation, low mental stress, and variability of practice. Students will have many opportunities to develop specific skills such as catching, throwing, kicking, and dribbling while playing the games in this chapter.

COMBINED APPROACH TO TEACHING A SKILL

Skill: Any chosen skill

Equipment: According to the choice of skill

Description: I am including the combined approach to teaching skills because of its direct relationship with the ideas presented in this book, especially the schema theory of discrete motor skill learning (see chapter 1).

➤ The combined approach is composed of four parts: free exploration, guided exploration, progressive problem solving, and specific instruction. In this way, students move organically from freely exploring a skill to receiving specific instruction.

➤ Following is an example of the use of the combined approach in a jump rope lesson:

1. Free exploration—Students jump rope freely for a couple of minutes.

2. Guided exploration (few restrictions)—Invite the students to explore the many ways they can jump: forward, backward, very slowly, alternating feet, two feet together, with a partner.

3. Progressive problem solving—Offer a few questions, challenges, or problems that will lead the students toward the desired skill, while still avoiding explanations and demonstrations (e.g., "Choose your favorite way of jumping and focus on keeping your upper body very straight").

4. Specific instruction—Demonstrate and teach, showing students how to jump keeping their feet together, how to make only one jump for each turn of the rope, how to turn the wrists only, and so on.

EQUIPMENT FUN

SKILLS   All sorts of manipulative explorations

EQUIPMENT   10 to 12 stations (marked by hula hoops on the floor), each with one piece of equipment or a complementary pair, if necessary; fun music

FORMATION   One pair of students at each station (one or two groups can have three students if necessary)

DESCRIPTION   The idea is to encourage students to develop personal relationships with all sorts of equipment so they can explore the many ways to use it.

> Allow students to play freely with the equipment at each station.
> Permit any sort of use, as long as it involves every student in the group. Groups may make up a game or any sort of unstructured activity using the equipment.
> Make sure that the play is safe and never aggressive.
> After a few minutes at their stations, groups rotate clockwise to the next station.

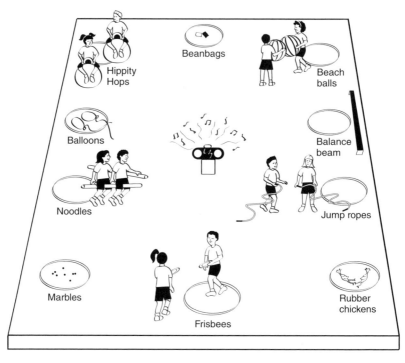

EQUIPMENT CHALLENGE COURSE

SKILLS   All sorts of manipulative explorations

EQUIPMENT   10 to 12 stations (marked by hula hoops on the floor), each with one piece of equipment or a complementary pair, if necessary

FORMATION   Pairs

DESCRIPTION   This activity builds on the preceding one, Equipment Fun; however, you determine the manipulative skill students practice.

> ➤ The stations are set up in a large circle around the gym or playing area, each with the necessary equipment for the challenge.
> ➤ Examples of manipulative challenges include various ways of balancing a wand, an elbow beanbag flip, tossing a beanbag into a bucket, jumping rope nonstop, hula-hooping nonstop, dribbling a ball around the body, hitting to keep a beach ball (or a balloon) in the air, batting a balloon with an empty water bottle, foot juggling a ball attached to a string.
> ➤ After a few minutes at their stations, groups rotate clockwise to the next station.

EQUIPMENT EXPLORATION

SKILLS   Open manipulative exploration; cooperation; social skills

EQUIPMENT   Your choice

FORMATION   Groups of three

DESCRIPTION   This activity allows students to experiment and develop their own personal relationships with equipment normally used in a gym setting, before being expected to use it in a particular way.

> ➤ Divide the class into groups of three, and set up as many equipment areas as you have groups. Each area should include the same three pieces of equipment (e.g., 10 sets consisting of one jump rope, one hula hoop, and one ball; or seven sets consisting of one baton, one scooter, and one beach ball).

> ➤ Place one group in each equipment area and instruct them to play freely with the equipment, although explain that the ultimate goal is to develop a game or activity to share with the class later.

> ➤ A 15-minute period seems to be ideal for the entire activity; additional time might be needed for sharing ideas.

KICKING FEAST

SKILL Kicking

EQUIPMENT One foam ball (or light soccer ball) for each pair of students

FORMATION Partners face each other on opposite sidelines of the gym or playing area.

DESCRIPTION This activity greatly exemplifies the application of the schema theory when teaching children, especially as it pertains to the necessity of high variability of skill practice.

> ➤ Partners kick the ball back and forth to each other using your command or according to the ideas presented in the Variations section.
> ➤ Students may not kick or distract themselves with other students' balls.
> ➤ The object of this activity is to kick the ball as many different ways as possible. Remind students regularly to alternate feet.
> ➤ Examples: with toes; with the inside of the foot; with the outside of the foot; with the heel backward; drop, bounce once, and kick; drop-kick before the ball touches the floor, hitting the ball on the laces; with the thigh; lying on one's back with one's head toward the partner, toss the ball over the foot and kick; kicking backward over the head; kicking lying on one's side; toss up, jump, and kick; spin and kick.

VARIATIONS

> ➤ Let students kick freely for a few minutes, asking them to try all imaginable ways of kicking to each other.
> ➤ Students kick to each other, aiming at making the ball go between their partners' legs. Partners stand still across the gym or playing area with their legs open.
> ➤ Invite students to raise their hands with suggestions for the class to try. Have the class try each idea for up to one minute.
> ➤ Give each pair a unique type of ball and have the pairs move their balls to the next pair on their right after a couple of minutes of playing. Examples include balls of different sizes, a large beach ball, a tennis ball, a deflated ball, a football, a very bouncy ball, a table-tennis ball, and a cage ball.

THROWING FEAST

SKILLS   Throwing and catching

EQUIPMENT   Smaller foam balls; various safe throwing objects (see variations)

FORMATION   Partners face each other on opposite sidelines of the gym or playing area.

DESCRIPTION   This activity borrows from Kicking Feast. The goal is to throw as many different ways as possible.

> Partners throw the ball back and forth to each other using your command or according to the ideas presented in the Variations section.

> Students may not catch or distract themselves with other students' balls.

> Remind students regularly to alternate hands.

> Examples: twist and shoot; jump and shoot; from behind; using two hands; alternating hands; hook shot; under the legs; backward with two hands; backward under the legs, using both hands; underhand; overhand; sitting down; chest shot while sitting down; lying down; sitting with one's back toward the partner and shooting overhead; as high as possible; step and shoot; step with the opposite foot and shoot.

VARIATIONS

> Allow students to throw freely for a few minutes, inviting them to try all imaginable ways of throwing to each other.

> Invite students to raise their hands and suggest ideas for the class to try. Let them try each idea for up to one minute.

> Give each pair a unique type of ball and have the pairs move their balls to the next pair on their right after a minute of playing. Examples include balls of different sizes, beach balls, a swim noodle, a foam Frisbee, a beanbag, a deflated ball, a soft football, a very bouncy ball, a table-tennis ball, and a cage ball.

> Divide the throwing into the three dimensions of movement: space (high, low, medium, overhand, underhand, under legs); time (fast, slow, run and throw, jump and throw); and force (very hard with two hands, with one hand, very soft throw, hard with left hand, very hard with right hand).

MY FAVORITE TRICK

SKILLS Catching; tossing; kicking; bouncing

EQUIPMENT Playground balls or foam balls

FORMATION Pairs, groups of four to six, or the entire class playing together

DESCRIPTION

> ➤ Students take turns showing a favorite trick, or ball skill, to their groups or the class.

> ➤ After the group executes the trick a few times, a new student takes the lead.

> ➤ Emphasize the concept of personal best and the harmlessness of just trying a skill even though they may not be able to replicate it exactly.

> ➤ You can establish categories for an extra challenge, such as performing using only the hands, using only the legs and feet, using any body part, while standing, while sitting, while walking, while running, against the wall, and while passing to a partner.

VARIATION This activity may also be done using any other kind of safe equipment.

10 WAYS OF GETTING THE BALL ACROSS

SKILL Open exploration of locomotor and manipulative skills

EQUIPMENT Playground balls

FORMATION Students stand side by side at one end of the gym or playing area, each with a ball.

DESCRIPTION This is a fun warm-up activity that emphasizes variability of practice. Encourage creativity.

> ➤ Have students cross the gym or playing area 10 times, each time performing a different task with the ball or carrying it in a unique way.

> ➤ Praise and encourage challenging ideas. Tell students that they should not simply hold the ball in their hands while crossing. They may borrow ideas from their peers.

> ➤ Remind students to keep track of the number of crossings and not to repeat any ideas.

Children absolutely love to play with objects, toys, and equipment. Let them experiment with lots of equipment and in many ways. Activities such as 10 Ways of Getting the Ball Across will defy any teacher's attempt to be as creative as children can be. The results of providing plenty of opportunities for organized free exploration with the equipment will be highly skilled and confident children using these same objects in future activities.

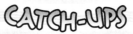

CATCH-UPS

SKILLS   Eye tracking; tossing and catching

EQUIPMENT   Several different objects, such as balls of various sizes, rubber chickens, beanbags, Frisbees—anything that is not too heavy or that won't cause injuries

FORMATION   Groups of five or six

DESCRIPTION   This game was developed by my students, and they have a great time playing it.

> ➤ Each group stands in a circle with one player in the middle.
> ➤ Each player around the circle holds an object; the player in the middle is empty-handed.
> ➤ At the count of three, the players toss their objects up and toward the center.
> ➤ Players try to catch an object, but because there are more players than objects, one player is left without one each time; that player goes to the center.
> ➤ A player who is left empty-handed twice in a row has to perform a task that the group decides, something simple, such as one lap, some jumping jacks, or three push-ups or sit-ups.
> ➤ If two players catch an object at the same time, they quickly play Rock, Paper, Scissors to determine who gets it.

TIP   Remind students of the importance of being aware of their movements toward the objects. Because they will be looking up to catch them, they may not see an approaching player.

TACTILE CHALLENGE

SKILL   Tactile awareness

EQUIPMENT   Many objects of different sizes and shapes

FORMATION   Pairs

DESCRIPTION   This activity previews later lessons on catching technique or any skill requiring fine motor dexterity.

> ➤ Place all the objects in the center of the playing field.
> ➤ One partner is sitting a few steps away from the objects with her back to them and her hands open and behind her back.
> ➤ The other partner chooses one object from the center and places it in the partner's hands. Keeping the object behind her back, the partner touches it to learn its shape, size, texture, and weight.
> ➤ The other partner then returns the object to the center and takes the place of the sitting partner, who now goes to the center to try to find the object she held.
> ➤ To maintain a reasonable challenge, each player should have only one chance to find the object.

FUN WITH HOOPS

SKILL   Open manipulative exploration

EQUIPMENT   One hula hoop for each student; 1 foam ball for one of the stations

FORMATION   Pairs of students and 10 to 12 activity stations. Each station has two to three hula hoops and a sign indicating the activity to be performed with the hoop.

DESCRIPTION   This activity also builds on the idea of providing plenty of opportunities for movement exploration. Highly agile and movement-creative young children should always be preferred to skill-confined ones.

> ➤ As with Equipment Challenge Course, set up 10 to 12 fun challenges with hula hoops. A sign at each station with short, clear instructions can help.
> ➤ Activity examples:
>> 1. Spin the hoop on the floor (by holding it vertically on the floor and spinning) and try to jump in without touching it.
>> 2. Same as item 1, but jump in and out without touching the hoop.
>> 3. Toss the hoop lightly over your head, horizontally, and stand under it so that it passes over your body.
>> 4. Roll the hoop on the floor, with a vigorous and fast backspin to make it come back.
>> 5. Spin the hoop at different parts of the body.
>> 6. With a partner, trap a ball between your foreheads and try to step through a hoop (picking it up from the floor) without dropping the ball.
>> 7. Toss a hoop gently to you partner, vertically; catch with two hands, away from your face.
>> 8. Use the hoop as a jump rope.
>> 9. Roll the hoop and go through it.
>> 10. Stand inside one hoop with your partner. Keep it at waist level and move around in different ways, without holding the hoop or letting it fall.
>> 11. Roll the hoop across the gym or playing area to your partner.
>> 12. Have your partner hold the hoop vertically, touching the floor, while you find several ways to go through it. Switch places.

HULA GOALIE

SKILLS   Hula-hooping; tossing; hitting; blocking; eye–hand coordination

EQUIPMENT   Four hula hoops; four foam balls

FORMATION

> ➤ Divide the class into three or four groups.
> ➤ Each group stands in a circle, with one player hula-hooping in the middle.
> ➤ Players around the circle should be at least three big steps away from the one in the middle.

DESCRIPTION

> ➤ The player in the middle is hula-hooping while the ones around the circle toss the ball (gently, underhand), trying to make it go through the hula hoop.
> ➤ The player in the middle may stop the ball with his hands by hitting it away.
> ➤ The players around the circle may toss the ball at the hoop or pass it to another player around the circle.
> ➤ If a player succeeds at getting a ball through the hula hoop (while the player in the middle is hula-hooping), the players switch places.

TIPS

> ➤ Of course, not every student knows how to hula-hoop perfectly; give them plenty of support as they try their best to keep the hoop moving.
> ➤ Do not allow hard throws. The ball should be tossed gently and underhand.

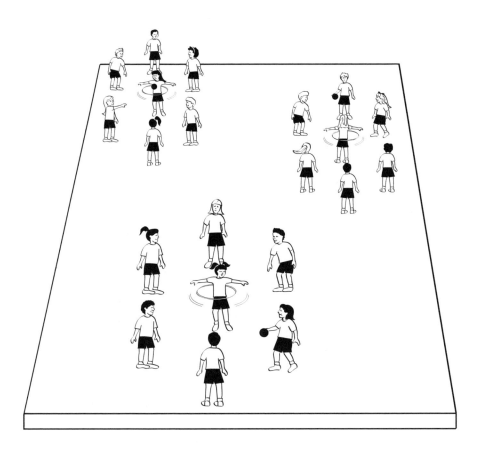

SUPER HOOPERS

SKILLS   Hula-hooping; running; tossing; dodging

EQUIPMENT   20 hula hoops; three beach balls

FORMATION

> ➤ Spread the hula hoops on the floor and have all but three students stand in them, one person per hoop.
> ➤ Three students are the taggers; they each hold a beach ball.

DESCRIPTION

> ➤ The game starts with players hula-hooping while taggers move among them.
> ➤ Each time a hula hoop stops or falls from the hips, that player has to move to another hula hoop, or run from the taggers until a hoop on the floor becomes available. While players are moving to other hula hoops, the taggers try to hit them with the beach balls before they can step into another hoop.
> ➤ When tagged, players switch places with taggers.

TIPS

> ➤ Taggers must keep moving; they cannot babysit next to a hula-hooper.
> ➤ Skilled players who are unlikely to drop their hula hoops may run to another hoop after 10 or 20 spins.
> ➤ Taggers may throw their beach balls, but they can tag only from the shoulders down. Tagging the face or head is not allowed.

Tagger

BLUP-UP

SKILLS   Cooperation; hitting; eye–hand coordination

EQUIPMENT   One beach ball

FORMATION   The entire class plays together.

DESCRIPTION

> The class spreads around the playing area and is given a beach ball.

> The object of the game is to keep the ball in the air for as long as possible, counting out loud each time someone hits it.

> When the ball is dropped, the player closest to the ball picks it up and restarts the game.

> Each restart of the game represents a challenge to beat the previous record.

> Players can hit the ball with any part of the body; however, explain that hands work best to make the ball go up instead of away from the group.

TIPS

> This is a cooperative effort. All students play for each other and not against each other. Remind them to do their best to help the group succeed.

> Ask students not to hit the ball away from the group.

BALLOON BLUP-UP

SKILLS   Eye tracking; eye–hand coordination; hitting

EQUIPMENT   One balloon for each pair of students

FORMATION   Pairs, one on each side of a line (or a jump rope on the ground)

DESCRIPTION   Students really enjoy this game, which is effective in developing eye tracking for future practice with balls. Use balloons as often as possible with young children.

> ➤ Partners stand on opposite sides of a line and hit the balloon across the line to each other, using any part of their bodies, keeping track of the number of hits they make in a row.

> ➤ A player may not hit the balloon more than once at a time. If the balloon does not go across the line, the partners restart counting.

> ➤ Partners should try to break their record each time they have to restart.

UP AND RUNNING

SKILLS Eye tracking; eye–hand coordination; hitting

EQUIPMENT Pinnies or rubber chickens; balloons

FORMATION Groups of five or six students

DESCRIPTION Balloons offer young children many opportunities for practicing the timing of hitting and catching. My students created this game during one of my yearly two-week sessions in which students make up their own games.

> ➤ The object of this game is for the players to keep the balloon up and not be tagged, and for the tagger (one in each group) to try to tag the last player who hit the balloon, before another player hits it.

> ➤ The tagger can wear a pinnie or hold a rubber chicken for identification.

> ➤ Other players scatter around and begin tapping a balloon into the air. Players have to hit the balloon and be mindful of where the tagger is so as not to be tagged.

> ➤ If the tagger tags someone who has just touched the balloon, before the next person hits it, the two switch places and the game restarts.

Tagger

HALF A DOZEN EGGS

SKILLS   Passing and catching; jumping jacks

EQUIPMENT   Three foam balls

FORMATION   Divide the class into three groups; each stands in a circle.

DESCRIPTION   This game works great with younger children.

> ➤ The group members throw a ball (an egg) to each other randomly and quickly.
>
> ➤ If the ball is dropped, the group has to perform one jumping jack.
>
> ➤ If the ball is dropped a second time, the group performs two jumping jacks, then three for three drops, and so on all the way to six, at which point they have broken half a dozen eggs.
>
> ➤ The group then performs six jumping jacks and forms a train (holding on to each other's waists), chugging around the countryside to buy more eggs (singing a song if desired).
>
> ➤ Once the group has returned to its spot, the game is restarted as previously until they break half a dozen eggs again.

TIPS

> ➤ Players must pass the egg nicely so no one gets hurt and everyone has a chance to catch it. Players may not toss it on the ground on purpose.
>
> ➤ A different player is the conductor each time the group must form a train.

THROWING SEVENS

SKILLS   Throwing; catching; hopping; balancing; jumping rope; hula-hooping; and more

EQUIPMENT   A basket of foam balls in the middle of the playing area

FORMATION   All players stand on a line (or see the variations that follow)

DESCRIPTION

> The game starts with players walking 30 steps along a line, without stepping completely off with their feet—or hopping 15 times on one foot.

> Players who step completely off the line must start counting again at zero.

> After taking 30 steps along the line, a player goes to the center and challenges another available player (who also has finished the 30-step task) with tossing and catching a ball seven times in a certain way without dropping it.

> The two players take turns challenging each other with different tossing and catching tricks.

> A player who drops the ball during these seven tosses must go back to the 30-step challenge and start again.

> The player who is challenging another player also has to toss seven times in demonstration. If he drops the ball during this demonstration, he has to go back to the line as well.

TIP Encourage students to be creative in the ways they toss and catch the ball. Suggest sitting, lying, or kneeling positions. Here are some ideas for tossing:

- Toss, clap, and catch
- Clap twice and catch
- Clap behind the back and catch
- Clap front and back and catch
- Clap under a leg and catch
- Clap under two legs and catch
- Toss, spin, and catch
- Toss, touch the floor, and catch
- Toss, touch the nose, and catch
- Toss, touch the ankles, and catch
- Toss against the wall, clap, and catch
- Toss against the wall, spin, and catch,
- Combine some of the preceding and catch

VARIATIONS Other tasks besides walking or hopping on a line can be used in this game. Examples include jumping rope 10 or 20 times, dribbling a basketball 20 times, doing jumping jacks, using a hula hoop, and doing 20 hippity hops. It is a great game to use to expose children to certain skills or have them practice skills they are working on.

TAP AND DROP

SKILLS Eye tracking, eye–hand coordination; overall agility

EQUIPMENT Buckets; tennis balls; balloons (beach ball for older grades)

FORMATION Groups of five players

DESCRIPTION

> Players stand in a large circle around a bucket, each holding a tennis ball.

> One player taps the balloon into the air and runs to the bucket to put the tennis ball in before the balloon hits the floor. Each player does the same in turn.

> The goal is to have every player place a tennis ball in the bucket before the balloon falls on the floor.

> Each time the entire group accomplishes the task, the group scores a point.

VARIATION Play the same game using a beach ball for a greater challenge.

SHOOTING STARS

SKILLS Frisbee tossing, hitting

EQUIPMENT Balloons and soft (preferably foam) Frisbees

FORMATION The class is divided into two groups. Each player in one group receives a balloon, and each player in the other group receives a Frisbee.

DESCRIPTION

- ➤ Players holding balloons roam freely around the area hitting and keeping their balloons in the air. When they are in the air, they are stars.
- ➤ Players with Frisbees toss them, trying to hit the balloons while they are in the air.
- ➤ When a Frisbee hits a balloon, the Frisbee player and the balloon player switch places.
- ➤ Players cannot shoot at balloons that are touching players' hands or that have fallen on the floor. Only stars can be shot at.

FRISBEE HUNT

SKILLS   Tossing; eye–hand coordination; hand dexterity

EQUIPMENT   Soft foam Frisbees; foam sticks (or empty water bottles), which are lightsabers

FORMATION

> ➤ Five or six taggers hold foam Frisbees.
> ➤ Other players are scattered around the playing area, each with a lightsaber.

DESCRIPTION

> ➤ Taggers toss the soft Frisbees at the running players, attempting to tag them from the shoulders down.
> ➤ Players use their lightsabers to try to block or hit the Frisbees away to prevent them from hitting their bodies.
> ➤ Whenever a player is tagged (i.e., the Frisbee touches any part of the body below the neck), she switches places with the tagger. No tag-backs.

KEEP THEM MOVING

SKILLS   Running; kicking

EQUIPMENT   Playground or foam balls (numbering three-fourths the number of students)

FORMATION   Balls are in the middle of the playing area; students stand around them ready to kick.

DESCRIPTION   The object of this game is to keep all the balls rolling for about two minutes using kicking skills.

> ➤ The entire class is playing against the teacher.
> ➤ Students are given 10 points at the start of every round of two minutes. For every ball that stops, they lose 1 point.
> ➤ Announce out loud during the game when a point is lost.
> ➤ When the time is up, if the students have lost more than 5 points (meaning, you saw more than five balls stop), you win. If the class loses fewer than 5 points, they beat you (cheers galore!).
> ➤ The game may be repeated two or three times, with an increasing number of balls for extra challenge.

KEEP IT CLEAN

SKILLS   Kicking; running

EQUIPMENT   Several foam balls

FORMATION

> ➤ Divide the class into two groups.
> ➤ Place groups on opposite sides of the gym.
> ➤ Players are not to cross the middle line.

DESCRIPTION

> ➤ Players scatter around their side of the gym. Each player has a ball and should be ready to kick it.
> ➤ On "Go," players on each side of the gym kick the ball to the players on the other side.
> ➤ Players cannot use their hands to hit or stop the ball. Kicking only.
> ➤ The goal is for each team to keep their side of the gym "cleaner"—that is, free of balls. Players should kick incoming balls back to the other side as soon as possible.
> ➤ The teacher blows the whistle after a minute or two and players freeze—no balls are to be touched at this point.
> ➤ Balls in each side of the gym are counted, and the group that has fewer balls—the side of the gym that is cleaner—scores a point.
> ➤ The game restarts as before.

TIPS

> ➤ The focus is the fun of kicking hundreds of times—not winning.
> ➤ When one team scores the other team applauds.
> ➤ Remind players that they are not to cross the middle line at any time.

SOCCER STOP AND DRIBBLE

SKILLS   Soccer dribbling and stopping

EQUIPMENT   One ball for each player

FORMATION   Scattered

DESCRIPTION

> ➤ Each player is given 10 points at the start of this game.

> ➤ On "Go," players walk or jog around the playing area trying to keep the ball as close as possible to their feet and stopping it before it touches anything or anyone.

> ➤ Every time a player's ball touches something, that player loses a point.

> ➤ Let students play for one minute each round, repeating it three times to give them a chance to improve.

> ➤ Prior to starting, demonstrate how to kick the ball lightly forward, alternating feet, and stopping.

NUTMEGS

SKILLS   Soccer dribbling; running

EQUIPMENT   One playground, soccer, or foam ball for each player (a sturdy foam ball is always preferred for younger children)

FORMATION   Scattered

DESCRIPTION   A nutmeg in soccer is passing the ball through an opponent's legs, running around the opponent, and continuing to dribble the ball.

> ➤ On "Go," players begin walking or jogging around the playing area keeping their balls close to their feet (soccer dribbling).

> ➤ Players try to lightly kick the ball through the legs of other players, going around them to continue playing with the same ball, keeping track of the number of times they succeed in doing that for two minutes.

> ➤ A player may not nutmeg the same person twice.

> ➤ Repeat the game two or three times to allow players to improve their records.

TIP   This game may be preceded by a couple of minutes of walking around trying to keep the ball under control and close to the feet; jogging; at the whistle, stopping the ball as fast as possible by lightly placing the foot on it; or kicking the ball against the wall with the inside of the foot.

CAVEMAN SOCCER

SKILLS   Kicking; soccer dribbling

EQUIPMENT   12 cones; several playground or sturdy foam balls

FORMATION

> Divide the class into three groups.

> Each group goes into one of the caves (a square of cones), which are placed far from each other.

> Several balls are placed in the center at an equal distance from each cave. There should be more balls than the number of players.

DESCRIPTION

> The game starts with each group in its respective cave.

> On "Go," all players run to the center and dribble one ball (using soccer skills only; no hands allowed) back to their caves.

> A player may either dribble a ball to his or her cave or try to steal a ball from players belonging to other caves, before they can kick it into their caves.

> When a ball is placed in the cave, it cannot be stolen by players from other groups.

> When all the balls are gone, groups count the number of balls they have captured, and the group with the most balls receives a nice round of applause (no points are needed).

> Balls are then returned to the center and the game begins again.

TIPS

> Students should follow the basic rules of safety in soccer: no pushing or grabbing when stealing a ball from an opponent.

> Once a ball has entered the cave, it cannot be stolen again even if it rolls out of the cave.

A traditional soccer drill is to have players dribble around cones. I often joke with my soccer-loving friends that the day I see a cone stealing a ball from a child, I will be convinced of its helpfulness during soccer practice. Dribbling around cones can be useful on the first attempt at conducting (dribbling) a ball with the feet. After that, children will benefit much more from actually *playing* and dribbling around each other. Dribbling and passing can be practiced without the dull routine of moving between cones. I developed the game Caveman Soccer as an example of that.

CROSS FIRE

SKILLS   Kicking; dodging; twisting; jumping

EQUIPMENT   Two foam balls (or any kind of soft or light ball)

FORMATION   Divide the class into two groups; half the players stand around a large circle (marked by lines), and the other half stand in the middle.

DESCRIPTION   My students adore this game. However, rules must be enforced to ensure fairness and the success of the game.

> ➤ The players around the circle have one light foam ball each, which they kick low, always close to the ground. The object is to hit the inside players below the waist.

> ➤ Players inside the circle may jump, dodge, or duck to avoid being hit.

> ➤ Players who are hit leave the circle and join the players around the circle to help with kicking.

> ➤ Introduce a second foam ball for the real cross fire, when fewer players are left in the middle. The game ends when one player is left in the middle.

> ➤ Restart the game with players assuming the opposite functions (i.e., players who started in the middle now form the larger circle, and vice versa).

TIPS

> Students should not kick the ball hard; using the inside of the foot and keeping the foot just off the ground will prevent the ball from going up and hitting faces. The players in the middle should be just touched by a ball, not whacked by it.

> Encourage players around the circle to try to keep the ball moving between them. They should not stop it before kicking. This will make the game more exciting.

> Watch for fairness. Make sure that players who are hit leave the middle to join those around the circle.

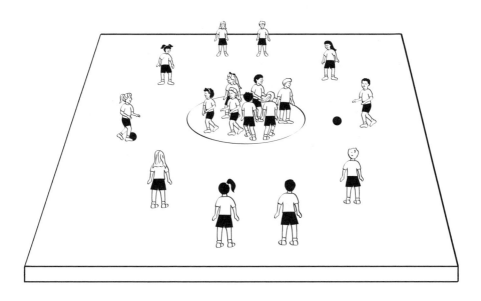

MEGA SOCCER

SKILLS   All soccer skills

EQUIPMENT   Foam ball, pinnies, indoor lines and walls

FORMATION

> Divide the class into two teams, and then divide each team into an equal number of goalies and forwards.

> Goalies stand behind a line that crosses the gym or playing area 10 feet from the back wall. Their job is to protect the entire back wall behind them.

> Forwards may not go into the goalies' area; they play only between the lines.

DESCRIPTION   In games containing some form of competition, players should believe that they all have an equal shot at winning. You can help accomplish this by explaining that the winning team is the one with the highest number of players scoring, not the highest score.

> This game is played like soccer, but the entire back wall is the net. If the ball hits the wall behind the goalies, from the height of their heads down, it is a goal. At that point the game starts from the center again.

> Goalies can use any part of their bodies, but they cannot punt to return the ball. They must throw it with their hands, passing it to a teammate playing as a forward.

> If a goalie crosses the line to catch a ball, the other team gets a free kick from the center of the playing area.

> Forwards cannot use their hands, and they cannot cross into the goalies' area. If a forward touches the ball with a hand, the other team gets a free kick from the center.

> Every few minutes, have goalies and forwards switch places.

TIP   Be firm with the rules. It sends students the message that they have to follow the rules to make the game fair for everyone.

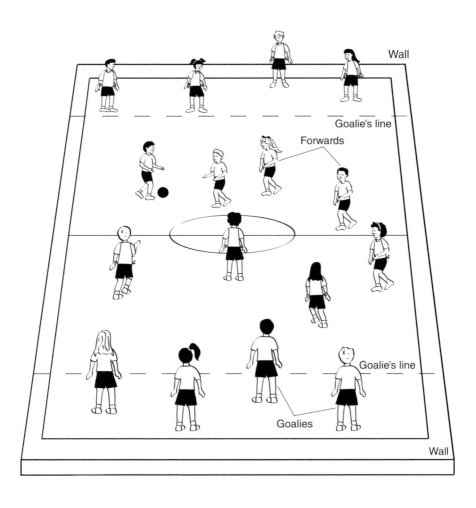

Wall

Goalie's line

Forwards

Goalie's line

Goalies

Wall

EXTREME SOCCER

SKILLS Kicking; tapping; hitting; heading; dribbling

EQUIPMENT Two large, light balls, preferably of different sizes

FORMATION Two groups, one on each side of the gym or playing area; no goalies

DESCRIPTION Extreme Soccer is my favorite way of playing soccer with younger children. They love the freedom of pretty much doing anything they want with the ball. Any way to move the ball is acceptable, except holding or picking it up.

> ➤ Everyone is both a player and a goalie. Anyone close to the net when the team is being attacked can stop the ball.

> ➤ Players can use any part of the body to hit the ball; however, they cannot hold the ball and run or walk as in American football.

> ➤ No one should catch the ball; only hitting, kicking, tapping, and dribbling are allowed.

> ➤ Do not keep track of points. Many goals happen constantly, and that is the objective. Emphasize nonstop fun and a great workout.

TAG PASS

SKILLS   Throwing; catching; running; dodging; eye–hand coordination

EQUIPMENT   About six foam balls

FORMATION

> ➤ Divide the class into three groups.
> ➤ Each group stands in a circle with one student in the middle.
> ➤ Players around the circle get a ball.

DESCRIPTION

> ➤ The players around the circle pass the ball around.
> ➤ The player in the middle (the tagger) tries to tag whoever is holding the ball before that player can pass it to someone else.
> ➤ A player who is tagged switches places with the tagger.

TIPS

> ➤ Players around the circle must pass balls nicely to each other.
> ➤ Players may not hit balls; they may only pass.
> ➤ Each group should stay in a circle formation.
> ➤ The circles must not be too widely spread out.
> ➤ After a while, add another ball to each group for extra fun.

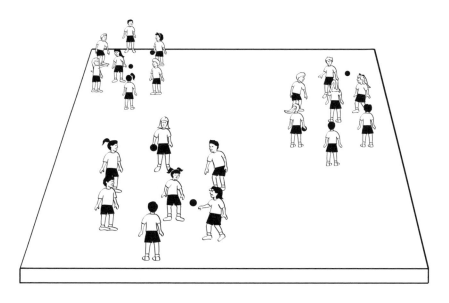

SCRAMBLE TAG

SKILLS   Throwing; catching; running

EQUIPMENT   Several small foam balls; three pinnies

FORMATION   Three taggers wear pinnies; three players start without a ball (these are the lifesavers); each remaining player has a ball.

DESCRIPTION

> ➤ The goal of the taggers is to tag a player who is holding a ball. At that point, the tagger and the tagged player switch positions.

> ➤ The lifesavers (three players without balls) can catch a ball thrown by someone who is being chased by a tagger. Once a lifesaver catches a ball, she can look for someone without a ball to pass it to.

> ➤ Sometimes a ball is left on the floor when a player forgets to catch it. When this happens, ask someone without a ball to pick it up.

> ➤ Players chased by taggers can run away or throw the ball to one of the lifesavers. However, when tagged holding a ball, they have to become a tagger and chase someone else (no tag-backs). Each player can have only one ball at a time.

VARIATION   Scramble Tag can also be played with soft Frisbees instead of balls.

Tagger

Lifes:

CHICKEN NOODLE

SKILLS   Throwing; catching; running

EQUIPMENT   Three foam noodles; around 15 rubber chickens, three pinnies

FORMATION   Three taggers wear pinnies; three players start without a chicken (these are the lifesavers); each remaining player has one rubber chicken.

DESCRIPTION   This game is played the same as Scramble Tag (see preceding description); the differences are that taggers use noodles to tag, and players pass rubber chickens instead of balls.

TIPS

> Players may not hide the chickens; it confuses taggers and life-savers.

> Taggers may not hit the players with the noodles; they should simply touch them.

ONE BOUNCE

SKILLS   Hitting; kicking; running; cooperation

EQUIPMENT   One bouncy ball, preferably not too hard or heavy

FORMATION   Scattered

DESCRIPTION   This is a fun and active warm-up and a great class-building activity as well. The goal is to bounce the ball on the floor only once before hitting or kicking it again.

> ➤ The class spreads around the gym or playing area, and one player hits or kicks a bouncy ball into the air.
>
> ➤ After that is pure fun: Players hit the ball hard with any part of the body and make sure it doesn't bounce twice. Players cannot hold or catch the ball.
>
> ➤ Once the ball bounces twice or someone fails to let it bounce first before hitting or kicking it, the counting restarts.
>
> ➤ Students keep track of their points, and every time the game restarts, they attempt to break their record.
>
> ➤ Students should count points out loud.

DRIBBLING WARM-UP

SKILLS   Dribbling; timing and rhythm

EQUIPMENT   One playground ball or basketball for each player

FORMATION   Scattered

DESCRIPTION   This game can be a good introduction to Dribble Tag, which follows. It was developed by my students. Its simplicity reminds us of the beauty of letting kids be kids during playtime, resulting in games such as this one.

> Students dribble freely around the area while walking, jogging, doing tricks, and so on.

> Whenever they want, they invite someone to trade balls with them without missing one bounce of the ball. They stand in front of each other, and on "Go," each player abandons his ball and runs to the other's ball trying to keep dribbling it before it bounces more than once.

> Students may keep track of how many different people they were able to trade with.

DRIBBLE TAG

SKILLS   Dribbling; running; catching; passing

EQUIPMENT   One rubber ball for each player

FORMATION   Scattered

DESCRIPTION

> Players dribble a basketball with one hand while trying to knock another player's ball away with the other hand.

> Players can knock a ball only while dribbling; they cannot hold their balls or leave them unattended while attempting the hit.

> Players can flee from each other only while dribbling; they cannot just grab the ball and run away.

> A player whose ball is knocked away must retrieve the ball, go to a predetermined area, and perform a task you established such as doing jumping jacks, doing sit-ups, or tossing the ball against the wall and catching it a few times.

VARIATIONS

> Players can take a break for a while by finding a partner to exchange balls with using passing skills. One partner passes with a bounce, and the other passes back with a straight pass to the chest. They may exchange passes for as long as they wish before rejoining the game.

> Other players may not stand close to passing partners, waiting for an opportunity to knock the ball away when the players rejoin the game—so-called babysitting.

WATCH THAT COLOR

SKILLS   Dribbling and running; hand dexterity; visual attention

EQUIPMENT   Several bouncy balls of the same color; four or five colored balls

FORMATION   Choose four or five players to be taggers and give them colored balls; give the remaining players balls of the same color (a distinct color from those of the taggers).

DESCRIPTION   This game builds on Dribble Tag (the preceding activity).

> ➤ The game starts with every player dribbling a ball.
> ➤ The taggers (with the colored balls) have to dribble with one hand while using the other hand to tag players without colored balls.
> ➤ Taggers must be dribbling when they tag someone. They cannot abandon their balls, tag, and go back to dribbling.
> ➤ When tagged, a player takes the colored ball and becomes the new tagger.
> ➤ There are no tag-backs.

BASKETBOOM

SKILLS Eye–hand coordination; basketball dribbling and shooting; cooperation

EQUIPMENT One balloon (plus extra ones); one rubber (bouncy) ball

FORMATION This game can be played in small groups or by dividing the class in two; it depends on the number of baskets available.

DESCRIPTION

> ➤ Players try to keep the balloon in the air while freely taking turns shooting the ball into the basket.

> ➤ Players try to keep the balloon in the air for as long as it takes for someone to score a basket.

> ➤ Because there is only one ball and one balloon per group, players must take turns, sharing the ball and the responsibility of keeping the balloon in the air.

> ➤ A player cannot attempt to shoot the ball in the basket twice in a row or before every teammate has been given a turn.

> ➤ Players are scattered around the basket area.

> ➤ Rules, such as no traveling or no double dribbling, can be introduced for extra challenge.

> ➤ Every time a player shoots the ball into the basket while the balloon is in the air, the group scores a point.

10 SECONDS OF LIFE

SKILLS   Running; dribbling

EQUIPMENT   Frisbees (or small rings); balls (or rubber chickens if using the variation); pinnies or something to identify taggers

FORMATION

> ➤ Three players are taggers.
> ➤ Spread Frisbees around the gym, and place one ball on each.
> ➤ Two or three Frisbees should not have balls on them.
> ➤ Players are spread around the area.

DESCRIPTION

> ➤ On "Go," taggers may chase any player who is not dribbling a ball.
> ➤ Players try to pick up a ball from a Frisbee before getting tagged.
> ➤ Players are safe from taggers while dribbling, but they can dribble only 10 times before they have to find an empty Frisbee to place the ball on and look for another ball. They may not use the ball they just put down.
> ➤ If tagged while running without a ball, a player switches places with the tagger.
> ➤ Taggers may not babysit. No tag-backs.

VARIATION   This game can be played with younger children who cannot dribble well yet. Simply place a rubber chicken on each Frisbee. Players are safe while holding a chicken for 10 seconds—hence the name 10 Seconds of Life.

INCLUSIVE BASKETBALL

SKILLS   Cooperation; dribbling; passing; shooting; stealing

EQUIPMENT   Three balls of different colors

FORMATION   Four small groups

DESCRIPTION   Because I believe that basketball is a great source of physical activity for young children, I have always wrestled with trying to make it more inclusive. Here is one version that has had positive results.

> ➤ Four small groups stand in each corner of the gym behind the back line.
> ➤ Three groups begin with a ball; one group has no ball.
> ➤ Each group has to score baskets in the opposite side of the court from where they start.
> ➤ Players in the group with no ball try to steal the ball from one of the other groups.
> ➤ Players can dribble only four times before they have to pass to another player or shoot.
> ➤ Each player can shoot only once before every member of the group has had a turn, or until the ball goes in (no layups).
> ➤ When a group scores a point, the players leave the ball under the basket and return to their corner, behind the line, to start over. Then, the group without a ball may pick it up.
> ➤ A group that has just scored and is without a ball now tries to steal a ball of another color (not the one it just scored with) from one of the other groups who are trying to shoot in the basket.

TIPS

> ➤ In each round (until a point is scored) the same player cannot shoot twice in a row, and nobody can dribble more than four times.
> ➤ Students keep track of their points (or not); the important factor is giving all players a chance to use all the skills involved in the game.

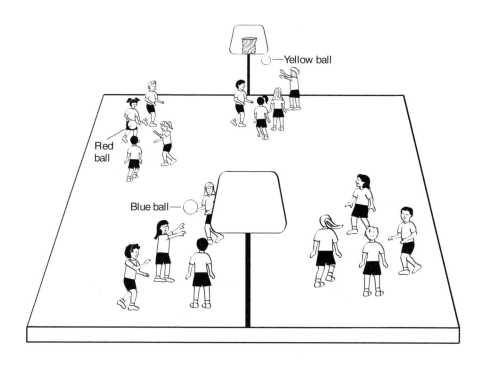

Yellow ball

Red
ball

Blue ball

TOGETH'AIR BALL

SKILLS   Cooperation; hitting; running

EQUIPMENT   One beach ball; a volleyball net or rope stretched across the gym or playing area at volleyball height

FORMATION

> The class is divided into two teams, one on each side of the rope.

> Each player on each team is given a number, from 1 to the equivalent number of players, so that there are two 1s, two 2s, and so forth, in the game.

DESCRIPTION

> Player 1 of any team starts the game by serving—that is, kicking the beach ball to try to make it go over the rope. Placing the beach ball about 20 yards (or meters) from the net, running toward it, and kicking under it in a scooping motion makes it go up.

> The other team tries to hit the beach ball back over the rope using any part of the body and hitting as many times as needed as long as the ball does not touch the floor.

> Each time the ball passes over the rope, not counting the serve (kick), both teams get a point.

> If the ball goes under the rope or touches the floor, the game restarts with player 1 on the opposite team kicking it over the rope.

> Each time the game restarts (with a serve), the player with the next number kicks the ball (player 2, then player 3, and so on). The goal is to break the previous record.

> Students can also keep track of the total number of hits over the rope during the class and keep the score as the class record. The next time they play the game, they can try to beat their class record.

Adapted, by permission, from T. Orlick, 2006, *Cooperative Games and Sports: Joyful Activities for Everyone,* 2nd ed. (Champaign, IL: Human Kinetics), 97-98.

FOOT TAG

SKILLS   Jumping; dodging; running; dynamic balance; throwing

EQUIPMENT   Six small foam balls

FORMATION   Six players receive a ball; the remaining players scatter around the area.

DESCRIPTION

> Six players are taggers and are given small foam balls.

> Taggers try to tag the remaining players by rolling the ball at their feet. The goal is to hit a player's foot (shoe); above the ankle does not count.

> If tagged, a player takes the ball and becomes a tagger. No tag-backs.

> Players jump or dodge the ball as taggers try to hit their feet.

TIPS

> The ball should be rolled, as in bowling, so as not to hit players too hard.

> Taggers should hand the ball to someone they tag, because players sometimes don't notice that they have been tagged.

> Disputes over whether the ball hit below or above the ankle should be decided using Rock, Paper, Scissors to avoid long arguments.

JUMP AND CATCH

SKILLS   Jumping rope; catching; tossing; eye–hand coordination; cooperation; physical multitasking

EQUIPMENT   Five long jump ropes; five foam balls

FORMATION   Divide the class into groups of four (or five if there is an uneven number of students).

DESCRIPTION   My students really enjoy this game, which challenges them to catch and jump at the same time.

> ➤ Optimally, this game it is played with four players on each team.
> ➤ Two players turn the jump rope.
> ➤ One player jumps.
> ➤ The fourth player (the thrower) stands in front of the jumper and gently tosses the ball to her.
> ➤ The jumper tries to catch the ball while jumping.
> ➤ The thrower throws the ball five times. If the jumper catches three or four out of five throws, the group gets one point. The jumper must keep jumping after catching the ball, or at least complete one more jump for the point to count.
> ➤ If the jumper catches all five throws, the group gets two points.
> ➤ After five throws, the players rotate positions. Everyone plays every position before the game is over.
> ➤ Points are assigned to the group, not individually.

TIPS

> ➤ The thrower waits for one full jump before tossing the ball to the jumper.
> ➤ Rope turners should turn the rope slowly and wide so as not to make jumping too difficult for their teammate.
> ➤ Remind the students that each person is important for the success of the group, and they should all do their part as best as they can.

DUNK OR HOP

SKILLS   Shooting; sack hopping

EQUIPMENT   One sack; two cones; one rubber ball; two buckets; several hula hoops

FORMATION

> Divide the group into two teams, A and B.

> One player (the shooter) stands between two cones at one open end of a large oval-shaped circle of hoops on the floor. The shooter holds the ball and has a sack on the floor next to her.

> Inside the circle are two buckets—one about 10 feet (3 meters) from the shooter and the other 20 to 30 feet (6 to 9 meters) from the shooter.

> The circle of hoops should not be too close to the buckets.

> Teams are in alternating positions in the hoops—that is, if a player from team A is the first shooter, the player to her right inside the hoop will be one from team B. The pattern should be A, B, A, B, and so on.

DESCRIPTION   I believe this game is one of the best I've developed. It works for children at any skill level, and despite the competitive aspect, everyone has an equal shot at winning. This game often ends up in a tie.

> Following the formation described, the player between the cones (from team A) tries to throw the ball into the closer bucket. If the ball goes in, the player advances to the hoop on the right and all other players advance (rotate) to the next hoop on their right.

> The player in the last hoop becomes the next shooter (from team B).

> If the shooter misses the bucket, she must get into the sack and hop around the outside of the hoops the other players are standing in. Meanwhile, players from team B try to get the ball in the bucket before the hopping shooter reaches the cones. If they succeed, they prevent team A from scoring. If the hopping shooter gets to the cones before team B gets the ball in the bucket, she scores a point for team A.

> Team B players must have two feet inside the hoop when shooting the ball at the bucket. If they miss, they can come out of the hoop to retrieve the ball, but they may only shoot from inside the hoop. They keep trying until the shooter completes the lap.

> Once the shooter reaches the cones, she advances to the hoop on the right and everyone rotates again.

> If the shooter who misses belongs to team A, only team B can throw the ball in the bucket, and vice versa.

> Points are awarded in the following manner: Only a shooter can score. If the shooter gets the ball in the bucket, his team gets a point. If he finishes the sack lap before the other team shoots the ball in the bucket, he also scores a point. However, if the opposite team gets the ball in the bucket during the sack lap, that team does not score a point. It simply prevents the shooter from scoring a point for his team. Now the players rotate counterclockwise, and a player from the opposite team has a chance to score.

TIPS

> Players shooting at the bucket must have both feet inside the hoop.

> Make sure the shooter is hopping and not running inside the sack during the lap.

> The game continues until everyone has had a chance to be the shooter.

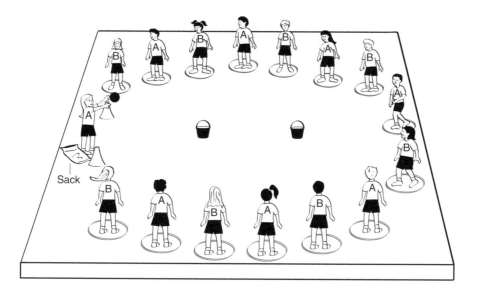

TOWEL BALL

SKILLS   Cooperation; synchronization; force control

EQUIPMENT   Large towels; one rubber ball; a rope or net stretched like a volleyball net

FORMATION

> ➤ Divide the class into two groups, one on each side of the net.
> ➤ Give each pair of players a towel.

DESCRIPTION

> ➤ The players use the towel to try to throw the ball over the net.
> ➤ Each time the ball is passed over the net and another pair across the net catches it before it touches the ground, both teams score one point.
> ➤ Players must throw the ball from where they catch it. They are not allowed to catch, walk over to the net, and shoot.
> ➤ If the ball bounces on the ground, the game continues with players catching it after the bounce and throwing it over the net.
> ➤ If the ball goes under the net, the opposite team restarts the game.
> ➤ Each team can make as many attempts as needed to get the ball over the net.

TIP   Players should always use the towel, not the hands, to throw and catch the ball.

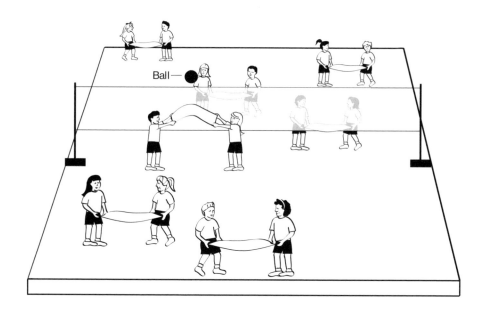

Ball

MARBLES

SKILLS   Fine motor skills; social skills

EQUIPMENT   One marble for each player

FORMATION   Groups of three or more players; played on smooth dirt ground

DESCRIPTION

> ➤ Players take turns shooting marbles from behind a shooting line attempting to get them into a small hole in the ground about 15 feet (or about 5 meters) away.

> ➤ If the marble does not go into the hole, the player has to wait for her next turn and shoot the marble from where it stopped.

> ➤ After one player shoots the marble in the hole, the others keep playing until only one is left.

> ➤ The game then restarts from the shooting line.

TIPS

> ➤ Wrap the index finger around the marble; place the thumb under the marble with the thumbnail touching it.

> ➤ Flick with the thumb. Do not throw the marble by using any arm movement.

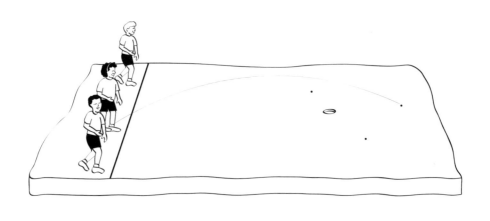

EGGS IN THE BASKET

SKILL   Throwing

EQUIPMENT   A bucket of used tennis balls

FORMATION   A bucket in the middle of a circle of cones or floor lines; children play together from behind the cones or lines.

DESCRIPTION   This is a fun warm-up for young children. My students love this cooperative game, always reminding me that sometimes simpler is better.

> ➤ Place the bucket in the middle of the circle and scatter the balls on the floor.
> ➤ Each student picks up a tennis ball, stands behind the circle's line or cones, and tries to toss the ball into the bucket.
> ➤ Students can go into the circle to retrieve a ball, but they can shoot only from behind the line.
> ➤ Time how long it takes the students to get all the balls into the bucket. At that point, begin a new round, challenging them to break their record. Play about three times.

Teacher with timer

CHAPTER

6

Stability Activities and Games

"**S**o, let's talk about stability . . . balance, you know?" I said to the first-grade class. "Can anyone tell me something about balance?" As always, I was looking for the easiest way to convey this concept to the students. A student called out, "Balance is not falling!" And I thought *I* could teach!

Although the primary goal of the games and activities in this chapter is the development of static and locomotor balance, this goal is achieved while incorporating manipulative and locomotor skills as well. As with the previous chapters, cooperation, variability of practice, and brain research on emotions and learning inform the games and activities in this chapter.

It is generally challenging to develop exciting and active games focused on such a specific concept as balance. This chapter attempts to do just that, given the importance of good balance for children's successful participation in any physical activity.

BALANCE DAY

SKILLS Various balance stunts

EQUIPMENT None

FORMATION Scattered

DESCRIPTION This can be one of the first balance activities of the year. It offers a combination of challenging and basic balance stunts. Remind students to stay as still as possible for three to five seconds during the stunts that call for stillness.

> ➤ Kneel down while standing on one foot.
> ➤ Do the same as the preceding, but then stand back up on one foot.
> ➤ Swing from your heels to the very tips of your toes.
> ➤ Swing heel-to-toe on one foot.
> ➤ Standing, lift one foot off the floor by bending the knee. Now lean forward and touch the toes of the foot that is on the floor. Do the same with the other leg.
> ➤ Grab one foot and bring it up to your forehead while standing still on the other foot. Switch feet.
> ➤ Standing up, cross one leg over the other knee (to make the shape of the number 4). Now pretend to sit down on your favorite chair to read a newspaper—bending the knee of the supporting leg. (This is a very challenging stunt enjoyed by all.)
> ➤ Find a personal space away from others. Now jump, spin in the air, and land on both feet.
> ➤ Do the same as the preceding, but freeze when you land.
> ➤ Do the same as the preceding with your eyes closed.
> ➤ Donkey kick—With both hands on the floor, raise both legs back and up together in a kick.
> ➤ Do the donkey kick, but try to finish the kick standing up.
> ➤ Sitting on the floor, stretch out your legs and raise them off the floor while holding your arms out at your sides. Balance on your buttocks only.
> ➤ Squat on your toes and straighten one leg out in front. Sit on the heel of the other foot.

BALANCE WARM-UP

SKILL Transition between dynamic to static balance

EQUIPMENT None

FORMATION Scattered

DESCRIPTION

> ➤ Choose a locomotor movement such as running, skipping, galloping, speed walking, slow motion running, dancing funny, walking funny, doing an animal walk, or doing a mummy walk. Have the students move around the area performing this movement.

> ➤ At each signal—a whistle—the students stop, and, taking one of the following balance positions, which you described before they started moving, they will: freeze; stop on one foot; one foot one knee on the floor; one foot one hand on the floor; one knee one hand; two knees only (no feet); one foot one finger; one knee one finger; two knees and forehead; back only touching the floor; heels only; tiptoes; one tiptoe, one heel; one heel only; squatting; scale; bridge; candle stick.

> ➤ After each stop in one of the positions, choose a different locomotor movement for the students to perform until the next signal.

BALANCE SCULPTURES

SKILLS   Balance; social skills

EQUIPMENT   None

FORMATION   Groups of four or five

DESCRIPTION   This is a good activity for calming students down while also helping them develop stability. Students in the early grades love to show off their creativity here. They can't wait to show me the new balance sculptures they made up before they crumble on top of each other and get a big laugh.

> ➤ Groups create static balance structures using every member of the group.

> ➤ Each person in the structure must be connected to at least one other group member.

> ➤ Encourage students to take turns talking and listening fully to others when planning structures.

WHEELBARROW

SKILLS   Balance; locomotion

EQUIPMENT   None

FORMATION   Pairs. One student in a push up position and the other holding his or her legs up, allowing that student to walk on hands.

DESCRIPTION   I can't say enough about the value of giving students a five-minute wheelbarrow warm-up with a partner. The activity is simple, no equipment is needed, and it's amazingly enjoyable. There is no need to foster competition; simply ask students to have fun and switch places whenever they want. Sometimes they organize a race, but because that is not the focus, laughing becomes the most prominent feature. Try it.

CROSSING BRIDGES

SKILL   Dynamic balance

EQUIPMENT   Cones; floor lines

FORMATION   Pairs or groups of three

DESCRIPTION

> ➤ Each group marks off a 10- to 15-foot (about 3- to 5-meter) "bridge" on a floor line, using two cones to indicate the beginning and end of the bridge.

> ➤ One student comes up with a way to cross the bridge and demonstrates it. Others in the group follow.

> ➤ Students try to stay completely on the line, whether they are crossing on their knees, crawling, jumping, or hopping. If a body part in use touches a bit off the line, that's OK as long as most of it is on the line.

> ➤ Remind students that the "river" below is full of crocodiles!

> ➤ Encourage creativity in coming up with a variety of ways to cross their bridge.

NOT ON THE LINE

SKILL   Balance

EQUIPMENT   Floor lines

FORMATION   Students begin standing on the line.

DESCRIPTION   This activity is similar to Balance Day (see page 138). It can serve as a warm-up to help students develop balance, or it can complement another balance activity. The goal in each of the following stunts is not to touch the floor line:

> ➤ Run around the gym or playing area freely without stepping on a line.
> ➤ Run following the lines without stepping on them.
> ➤ Walk across the line, crossing one leg over the other without touching the line.
> ➤ Hop twice on each foot on either side of a line without touching it.
> ➤ Walk backward over a line without touching it.
> ➤ Jump freely over and around a line without touching it.
> ➤ Dance freely to music over a line without touching it.

PARTNER GYMNASTICS

SKILLS   Balance; cooperation

EQUIPMENT   None

FORMATION   Partners equally matched in size

DESCRIPTION

> ➤ Choose partners of approximately the same size and strength for best results.

> ➤ The following nine ideas for partner exercises and gymnastics movements will help students improve balance and muscle strength:

>> 1. Handshake Rescue—Partners squat facing each other, hold each other's right hands as in a handshake, lean slightly backward, then release their right hands and try to catch each other's left hands before completely falling backward.

>> 2. Push-Up Handshake—Partners face each other in a push-up position on the floor. They execute one push-up, then shake each other's right hands; perform another push up, then shake each other's left hands; and continue for a specific number of push-ups.

3. Pulling Under Legs—One partner is standing up with legs spread apart. The other partner lies on the floor behind the standing partner, belly down with arms stretched forward so his hands are between his partner's feet. The standing partner grabs the other's hands and drags him under his legs as far as possible. They switch positions and restart.

4. Russian Dance—Partners squat facing each other and holding hands. They both stretch their right legs forward and then, with a small jump, bring the right legs in and stretch the left ones. They continue in this manner. This is somewhat challenging.

5. Partner Rolls—Lying on the floor on their backs, head to head, and holding hands stretched above their heads on the floor, partners roll together around the gym or playing area.

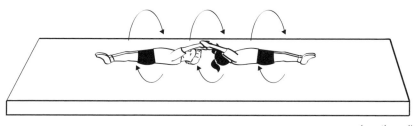

(continued)

(continued)

6. Lift the Potato Sack—One partner sits firmly on the floor hugging her knees to her chest. The other partner squats behind her, and, sticking her hands under her partner's armpits (from behind, never from the front), tries to lift her. Partners then switch places. Squatting before lifting is a must.

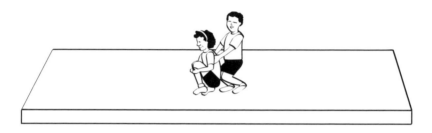

7. Rolling Bridges—This is my favorite one. Second- and third-graders and older students are able to accomplish it. Student 1 lies on the floor. Student 2 grabs his ankles in a push-up position, with arms firmly extended. Meanwhile student 1 grabs student 2's ankles and lifts him up above his body. Thus, student 2 is in the air over student 1. Now they slowly roll to one side still firmly holding each other's ankles and finish in opposite positions. They continue rolling slowly.

8. Getting Up Together—Partners sit on the floor facing each other, holding both hands and touching feet, knees bent. They try to stand simultaneously by pulling hands and pushing feet.

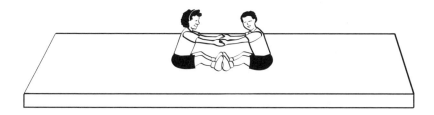

9. Back to Back and Up—Partners sit back to back on the floor leaning against each other. Their elbows are hooked and close to their bodies and their knees are bent so their feet are close to their bodies. They try to get up together without releasing their elbows or touching their hands to the floor; they rise only by pushing back against back, and up.

Adapted from T. Orlick, 2006, *Cooperative Games and Sports: Joyful Activities for Everyone,* 2nd ed. (Champaign, IL: Human Kinetics), 55.

SLOW MOTION ADVENTURES

SKILL   Balance

EQUIPMENT   None

FORMATION   Groups of four to six

DESCRIPTION   Moving creatively in slow motion challenges children and develops their balance skills. This is a static and locomotor balance activity; it gives students the opportunity to be creative in their movement and in their thinking.

> ➤ Each group makes up a quick story or action that can be depicted in movement.
> ➤ Every member of the group has to be included at all times.
> ➤ The group performs the short story in slow motion, striving to move as slowly as possible.
> ➤ The activity begins again with groups performing their stories to the other groups, or making up new ones.

BALANCE BEAM BALL

SKILL Balance

EQUIPMENT Balance beam; extra large beach ball, cage ball or large exercise ball

FORMATION Groups of two

DESCRIPTION Despite the apparent competitive nature of this game, it was developed by my students, and I recall some of the least sports-enthusiastic players having a great time playing it.

> ➤ The goal is to throw the opponent off balance by rolling the ball toward him or her.

> ➤ In this game, only one pair can play at a time. If not enough balance beams are available, other pairs can play different balance games while waiting for their turns.

> ➤ Partners balance on either end of the balance beam while rolling a ball back and forth to try to unbalance each other.

> ➤ If the ball rolls off the beam, the player who rolled it switches with a waiting player.

> ➤ A player who loses his balance and falls off the beam also switches with a waiting player.

> ➤ The game proceeds in this fashion with players taking turns.

HUMAN OBSTACLE COURSE

SKILLS   Balance; body awareness

EQUIPMENT   None

FORMATION   Divide the class into three small groups.

DESCRIPTION

> ➤ Each group forms a line of human obstacles, meaning that each student takes on a shape representing an obstacle. The first player in line has to go through, under, or over each obstacle.

> ➤ After the first player goes through the obstacle course, she stands at the end of the line and shapes her body into an obstacle; the player now in front of the line starts to go through.

TIPS

> ➤ The "human obstacles" may instruct the player going through the course on what to do, such as "crawl under," "jump over," and so on.

> ➤ Emphasize creativity, fun, and safety as the players use their bodies to create obstacle courses.

GROUP BALANCE

SKILL   Balance

EQUIPMENT   None

FORMATION   Groups of four

DESCRIPTION   Group members have to be connected while performing any stunt.

> ➤ Instruct the groups to find a balance position in which 10 body parts are touching the floor. Make sure your students are actually balancing, not just standing on two feet. Then have them progressively reduce the number of body parts in contact with the floor. First have them try the position with 9 body parts touching the floor, then 8, and so on. Two body parts may be the lowest number, to account for safety.

> ➤ Now have the groups create positions in which they are each connected to one other member and have only one body part touching the floor. To add to the challenge, mandate that each member has to have a different body part in contact with the floor.

BEANBAG HEADS

SKILLS   Balance; running

EQUIPMENT   About 16 beanbags

FORMATION

> Set up a small circle of cones in the middle of the playing area.
> Choose four taggers to stand outside the circle. They do not get beanbags.
> The remaining players go inside the circle and have beanbags on their heads.

DESCRIPTION

> Players inside the circle begin to speed walk randomly trying to keep their beanbags from sliding off their heads.
> Once a player has placed the beanbag on his head, he cannot touch it again until it falls.
> Players must walk fast, or else it is too easy to keep the beanbags on their heads.
> Once a beanbag falls, the player picks it up and, *holding it in her hand*, she runs out of the circle.
> A player holding a beanbag can be chased by the taggers and has to give the beanbag to the tagger if tagged.
> After tagging someone, the tagger goes into the circle to speed walk with the beanbag on his head. He becomes a "beanbag head."
> The player who lost the beanbag becomes a tagger and tries to tag other players.

TIPS

> Once the beanbag begins to slide off, a player cannot put it back with his hands.
> Taggers cannot babysit players—meaning, they cannot stand right next to a player waiting for her to drop the beanbag in order to chase her.

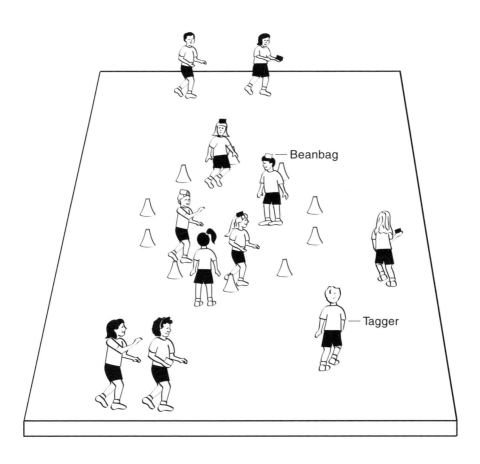

Beanbag

Tagger

SWINGING TREES

SKILLS   Running; heel-to-toe walking; balance

EQUIPMENT   About 20 "spots" (small plastic rings or hula hoops); four pinnies

FORMATION

> Choose four students to be taggers, and give them each a pinnie. Each tagger represent a wind—south, north, west, and east.

> The remaining players are "trees." They each take a "spot" standing inside the ring or hoop, and begin to swing, standing up, rocking from heel to toe.

DESCRIPTION   Present his activity once your students understand the concept of heel-to-toe walking.

> The trees swing continually while on a spot. Taggers may not tag them when they are swinging on a spot.

> Anytime they choose, trees may challenge the winds to tag them by running from one spot to another.

> Taggers may also tag trees that are standing in a spot but not swinging.

> If tagged, a tree is a fallen tree and sits on its spot (or the place it was tagged) until another tree saves it by lightly touching its head.

> After a few minutes, choose four other students to be winds (taggers).

TIP   Taggers may not babysit (stand next to a tree waiting for the player to run).

Children are much more willing to practice a skill when it's inserted into a game, or, better, if it's the main feature of a game. The concept of heel-to-toe walking is important for overall body balance, spine equilibrium, and blood flow to the brain. It counteracts toe walking, a common problem that increases neck tension. In Swinging Trees, children practice rolling their feet from heel to toe hundreds of times while having fun.

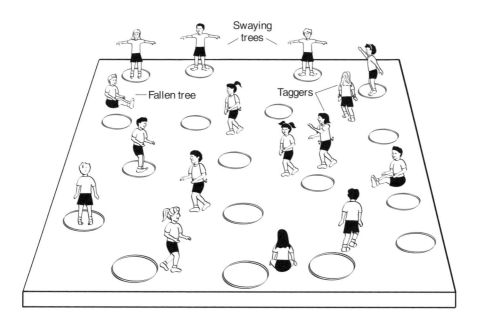

Swaying trees

Fallen tree

Taggers

NOSE AND TOE TAG

SKILLS   Balance; running

EQUIPMENT   Pinnies to identify taggers

FORMATION   About four players are taggers and wear pinnies; the remaining players are scattered.

DESCRIPTION   Like many games in this book, this game is a vehicle for practicing a skill—in this case, balance, by having students stand still for three seconds while holding one foot to the nose.

> ➤ Choose four or five taggers, and have them switch with other players every few minutes.

> ➤ When a player is tagged, he stops and slowly grabs one foot and brings it to his nose. (Students love to be told they will take a good sniff of their shoes.)

> ➤ Players must stand in this position for three seconds (see the following variations) and then are free to run again.

> ➤ Obviously, some students cannot bring their toes all the way to their noses, or balance in that position for three or more seconds. Accommodations and reassurances are necessary here. Emphasize their personal best.

VARIATIONS   The first time players are tagged, have them hold the position for three seconds; the second time, four seconds; the third time, five seconds; the fourth time, three seconds with each foot.

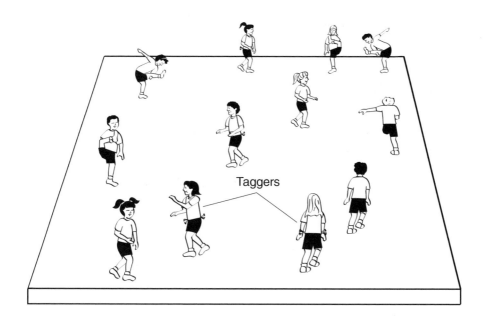

Taggers

MONKEY HUNTERS

SKILLS   Balance; running

EQUIPMENT   Five pinnies

FORMATION   Five or six students are monkey hunters and wear pinnies; the remaining students are monkeys.

DESCRIPTION

- ➤ Monkeys stand on a line balancing themselves on one foot while the other foot touches the opposite knee.
- ➤ Monkeys are safe from monkey hunters while in position on the line.
- ➤ Monkeys who lose their balance (even just touching the other foot to the floor) have to move to another line. Monkeys may also run to another line whenever they feel like challenging the hunters (although they may not simply run around). The main object of this game is balancing.
- ➤ When a monkey is running to another line, a hunter can tag her, in which case she has to sit down inside the circle in the middle of the playing area (the monkey cage) and perform monkey gestures.
- ➤ Other monkeys can try to save a tagged monkey by going in the monkey cage and lightly touching her head, at which point the monkey can go back to the game, balancing on a line again.
- ➤ After a few minutes, choose new hunters.

TIPS

- ➤ Monkeys cannot stay on the same line if they are losing their balance. Once they lose their balance, even slightly, they must move to another line.
- ➤ Monkey hunters cannot babysit—that is, stand right next to a monkey waiting for him to move to another line.

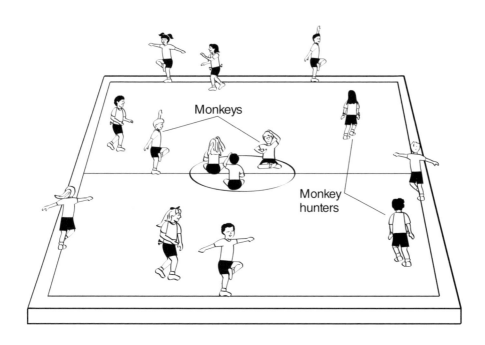

Monkeys

Monkey hunters

GROOVY SNAKES

SKILLS   Balance; slithering; running

EQUIPMENT   Four or five pinnies for taggers

FORMATION   Four or five taggers ("evil vultures"); one or two "groovy snakes"; the remaining players are runners ("mice").

DESCRIPTION   The important feature of this game is the balance stunt players perform once tagged.

> ➤ Evil vultures chase the mice. Once a player is tagged, she assumes a push-up position and lifts one hand and one foot off the floor. The hand and foot should be from opposite sides of the body for extra challenge.

> ➤ Groovy snakes slither under the tagged mice to save them, in which case they may run again.

> ➤ Taggers may not tag mice or snakes while they are performing the balancing task.

> ➤ After a few minutes choose new taggers.

CHAPTER

7

Combined Movement Activities and Games

The games and skill development activities in this chapter encompass more than one of the objectives presented in chapters 4, 5, and 6. Here locomotor, manipulative, and stability skills are combined to meet the pedagogical goals of this book. Some of the most interesting games are found here. For a truly great time with your students, try All for One or Two-Minute Challenge.

COOPERATIVE JIGSAW PUZZLE

SKILL   Any skill you choose

EQUIPMENT   According to the skill chosen

FORMATION   Four groups (of no more than five children)

DESCRIPTION   This is a physical education version of the traditional cooperative learning activity Jigsaw Puzzle, which I first encountered in the writings of Johnson, Johnson, and Holubec referenced in chapter 2.

> ➤ Give each group one skill or exercise to learn—to the best of their abilities. Every member tries to perform according to the group's understanding of the skill.

> ➤ Members who are unable to perform the skill at the agreed level should still be able to explain or teach it to others.

> ➤ After every group member has learned the skill, form new groups using one member from each original group.

> ➤ Members of the new groups take turns teaching the skills they learned in their original groups to their new group members.

> ➤ Numbering the original groups avoids wasting time. A member from group 1 teaches first, then one from group 2, and so on.

> ➤ Examples of skills to use: crossing a jump rope, balancing on the hands in a squatting position, cartwheel, baseball pitching.

MEMORY RIDE

SKILLS   Open movement exploration; attention; memorization

EQUIPMENT   None

FORMATION   Pairs

DESCRIPTION   Explain to students that they will be acting the way their brains act when remembering and repeating tasks.

> ➤ Partners freely move around the gym or playing area, making five stops at any place or object. At each stop they perform a movement, exercise, or skill of their choice.

> ➤ After they have made the five stops, the partners go back to the beginning and repeat their memory ride, making the same stops and performing the same tasks.

> ➤ Explain that this is the way the brain remembers things, by following the same path of neuronal connection for a given objective.

VARIATIONS

> ➤ Partners may perform their memory rides backward or add more stops for extra challenge.

> ➤ Provide equipment at the center of the playing area for manipulative tasks.

COOPERATIVE CORNERS

SKILLS   Any skill; cooperation; social skills

EQUIPMENT   According to the activity

FORMATION   Four small groups, one in each corner of the gym or playing area

DESCRIPTION   Because students take part in a variety of games, this activity can achieve several objectives at once. However, most important is to choose simple, cooperative games that can be played in a corner of the playing area and learned quickly after groups rotate.

➤ Give groups 5 to 10 minutes at each station; this seem to be enough time to assimilate the game and have fun.

➤ The following are examples of four cooperative corners:

1. Balloon Blup-Up (see chapter 5, page 91)
2. Students sit in a small circle, legs spread apart, trying to keep several balls rolling nonstop, and preventing them from going out of the circle.
3. Towel Ball. Two players hold the two ends of a towel and use it to shoot a ball to the other players in the group, who are holding another towel in the form of a net. Players toss and catch to each other.
4. Volley Orbit (page 179).

TIP   You can give students a variety of skill practice in a single session with this activity. Each time you use this activity, you can focus on different skills.

MOTOR MEMORY

SKILLS Choice of movement exploration; attention; social skills

EQUIPMENT According to the skill

FORMATION Groups of five or six students standing in a circle

DESCRIPTION You can use this activity as a fun stretching warm-up or to explore variability within any skill.

> Group members stand in a circle with enough space to perform the movement.

> Choose a skill or category of movement—for example, stretching.

> Have one student in each group demonstrate her favorite stretch (or any stretch she can think of). The rest of the group performs the stretch.

> The student on the right (or left) of the first student now demonstrates another stretch, and they all perform it, followed by the first stretch. Now the third student chooses a stretch, and after executing it, they again perform stretch 2 and stretch 1, and so forth. When every group member has demonstrated a stretch, choose another skill or category, or end the activity.

> This is also a good activity for practicing tossing and catching with balls, beanbags, and so on. You can also have students simply exploring their favorite exercises around the circle. In any case, the memory challenge is present.

Jumping jacks

Leg splits

Sit-ups

COUCH POTATO ACTIVITY

SKILL   Reinforcing neuronal pathway of any chosen skill

EQUIPMENT   Paper and pencil for each group

FORMATION   Groups of four

DESCRIPTION   Research on the brain informs us that when we think of an action, the same pattern of neuronal firing occurs in our brains as when we are actually doing it. This activity explores this concept by having students imagine the sequence of events of a skill, thus fine-tuning the pattern of neuronal firing before they actually attempt the skill.

> ➤ Assign one skill to each group (catching, throwing, kicking, shooting a basket, doing jumping jacks).

> ➤ The group sits down, and together its members describe on paper exactly how the skill is executed from beginning to end (it is crucial that they not attempt the skill yet).

> ➤ When the group has no more input to add, one by one each member tries to execute the skill by following the steps the group has written.

> ➤ The members not performing the skill check to see if what the performing member is doing matches what they have written. They make corrections to their description while helping the member who is performing the skill.

> ➤ This activity forces students to visualize, and consequently better understand, how their bodies move in any given skill. The learning results are extremely positive.

BOOK ACTION STORY

SKILLS   Various locomotor movements; general coordination and body awareness

EQUIPMENT   A children's book full of movements to act out

FORMATION   None

DESCRIPTION

> Read the story, pausing after each section, paragraph, or sentence that describes an action.

> Have students act out the part you have just read.

> After acting out this part, students gather to listen to the next part.

> Be sure to maintain control of the group. Students should have complete freedom (within safe guidelines) to move and make sounds during the acting part, and complete focus and attention during the reading.

SCULPTOR

SKILL   Cooperation

EQUIPMENT   None

FORMATION   Groups four to six

DESCRIPTION

> Choose one player to be a sculptor.
> The remaining players are pieces of clay that the sculptor is going to mold into a sculpture.
> The sculptor moves people's body parts into desired positions. Players should stay in position until the sculptor finishes the masterpiece.
> Choose a new sculptor.

TIPS

> Do not permit sculptors to use embarrassing positions.
> Encourage the sculptor to be creative, using sitting, lying down, and kneeling positions, not just standing.
> Remind the pieces of clay to be cooperative.

The sculpture

Sculptor

ACTION ADVENTURES

SKILLS Any locomotor movement; open movement exploration

EQUIPMENT None

FORMATION Scattered

DESCRIPTION As in the games Mutations (chapter 4, page 49) and Charades (page 174), Action Adventures allows children to explore their love of acting and imitation. In this activity, however, the action is nonstop, freer, and full of interactions as players come up with their own interpretations of the adventures while also observing and imitating others.

> ➤ Name a quick action adventure that the children can experience as though actually living through it. Every 30 to 45 seconds, suggest a new adventure.

> ➤ Some examples: moving through quicksand; being attacked by bees; sinking in a ship; practicing boxing or hitting a punching bag; being a cat chasing a mouse; building a house; fighting wildfires; rocketing to the moon; riding a wild horse; hitting a home run; gliding across a frozen lake.

MUSICAL TASK CARDS CIRCUIT

SKILL   Open movement exploration

FORMATION   Pairs

EQUIPMENT   According to the choice of tasks

DESCRIPTION   This activity provides the greatest variety of movement experiences.

> ➤ Set up a large circle of stations around the gym or playing area. Each station has a hula hoop on the floor with two or three task cards in it.

> ➤ Partners jog around the outside of the stations until the music starts. Then, they choose an unoccupied station, flip one card for the two of them, read the task printed on it, flip the card back over, and perform the task until the music stops.

> ➤ If, on arriving at a station a second time, the partners flip the same card they did last time, they are allowed to choose another card.

> ➤ Partners must perform the task near their station and not wander around the gym or playing area.

> ➤ Place any equipment needed for any of the stations (e.g., jump ropes, balls) in the middle of the gym or playing area.

> ➤ Task cards can include small drawings along with the name of the task for faster understanding.

> ➤ Examples of station tasks include rolling, becoming statues, clapping along with the music, tap dancing, chicken dancing, dribbling, hitting a balloon, hula-hooping, running very fast in place, doing jumping jacks, juggling beanbags, jumping rope with a partner, doing a favorite animal walk, doing a favorite stretch, doing a favorite exercise, and jumping and spinning.

Physical education teachers and coaches who want their children to practice many aspects of a sport simultaneously would benefit greatly from adapting the following activity, Musical Task Cards Circuit, to their goals. Upwards of 40 skills can be practiced in a single class or practice session. Some fun tunes can make the session even more enjoyable.

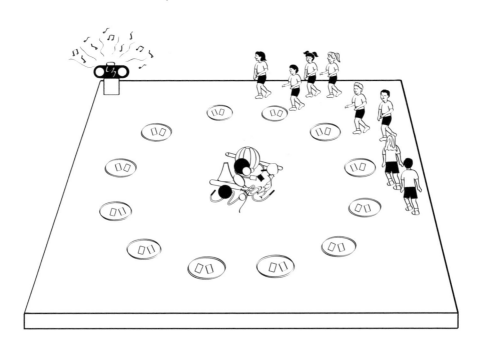

CHARADES

SKILLS   Various locomotor movements; open movement exploration

EQUIPMENT   None

FORMATION   Divide the class into two groups.

DESCRIPTION

> One group sits while you give the other group something to act out using only movements; no words or sounds are allowed.

> The group sitting down tries to guess what the other is trying to depict.

> After a few chances to guess (ask children to raise their hands if they think they know what the charade is), the groups switch places. Have the new acting group huddle close to you as you quietly tell them the new subject to act out.

> Here are some examples of charades that young children enjoy acting out: trees in the wind, a flat tire while riding a bike, ocean waves, last day of school, scuba diving, playing on a swing set, having a picnic and getting ants in the pants, ship floating on the water, building a house, riding a bumpy road, swinging from tree to tree, conducting an orchestra, parachuting, having snowball fights, sleep walking, sinking in quicksand, Santa getting stuck in the chimney, taming a lion, battling a snowstorm, making pizza, driving a garbage truck, making lemonade and selling it at a stand, getting ready for school in the morning, riding a bike and losing brakes downhill, parachuting and falling on a landfill, feeding the chickens and getting attacked.

PARTNER CHARADES

SKILLS   Various locomotor movements; open movement exploration

EQUIPMENT   None

FORMATION   Groups of no more than three

DESCRIPTION

> ➤ Partner Charades is played the same way as Charades, except that students provide the ideas to act out.
> ➤ Students will act and guess within their own groups of two and three.
> ➤ Students really appreciate this way of playing charades. Because the groups are small, they get to perform more often, and they feel a sense of ownership of the activity.

STORY OF MY LIFE

SKILLS Any locomotor movement; open movement exploration

EQUIPMENT None

FORMATION Scattered

DESCRIPTION This is another of my students' favorite activities.

> ➤ Invite students to act the way they think they acted when they were one, two, three, four, five, six, or seven years old.

> ➤ For every year of their lives, give students a maximum of one minute to act it out.

> ➤ Students should also portray the activities they remember doing at certain ages—for example, starting swimming lessons at four, taking ballet lessons at five, learning how to hit a baseball at three.

TWO-MINUTE CHALLENGE

SKILLS   General motor skills

EQUIPMENT   Stopwatch or regular watch

FORMATION   Scattered

DESCRIPTION   Give the students three simple tasks that they have to perform with as many other students as possible in two minutes. Following are some ideas, but feel free to make up your own.

> Examples

1. Shake hands; crawl under each other's legs; give a low-ten back to back to each other, under the legs (clapping both hands).
2. Shake hands; do two jumping jacks; jump and high-ten in the air.
3. Shake hands; spin around twice; lock elbows and hop around once.
4. Shake hands; do two jumping jacks; go under each other's legs.
5. Shake hands; do two push-ups; jump and high-ten in the air.
6. Shake hands; frog jump over each other; jump and spin.

> Remember that each three-task example is for a two-minute session.
> Students have to count how many partners they perform the three tasks with; they may not perform with the same person twice.
> In each new two-minute period (with three new tasks), students try to beat their previous record of the number of partners they performed with.

HUMAN MACHINES

SKILL   Open movement exploration

EQUIPMENT   None

FORMATION   Groups of four or five

DESCRIPTION   Groups try to move like machines, inventing a machine or acting out one they know.

> Everyone must be connected to someone's body part.

> All members must be moving (preferably, each in a different way)

> They must work together as a team, listening to and discussing ideas with each other.

TIPS

> Look out for ideas and machines that might not be safe.

> Remind students to explore many body positions, such as sitting, lying, and kneeling. Do not allow them to climb on top of each other—that is, no piggyback pyramids.

VOLLEY ORBIT

SKILLS   Cooperation; kicking; hitting

EQUIPMENT   One very large beach ball; two gym mats

FORMATION

> ➤ Place two mats in the center of the playing area. Half the students lie on their backs in a circle on the mats with their feet in the center.

> ➤ The remaining players stand in a circle about two steps from the mats.

DESCRIPTION

> ➤ The students lying on the mats try to hit the beach ball with their feet by raising their legs in the air while staying on their backs.

> ➤ The object of the game is to keep the ball in the air for as long as possible.

> ➤ Players standing in the circle around the mats are the supporting players. Their job is to hit the ball back over the mats whenever it leaves the circle. They should use two hands to make sure the ball falls nicely right over the mats so the others can resume hitting it with their feet.

> ➤ After a few minutes, players switch places.

> ➤ No points are scored. This is not a competitive activity. The goal is simply to enjoy it.

TIP   Players lying on the mats can protect their faces from the ball by placing their hands behind their heads with their elbows shielding their faces.

Adapted, by permission, from T. Orlick, 2006, *Cooperative Games and Sports: Joyful Activities for Everyone,* 2nd ed. (Champaign, IL: Human Kinetics), 104.

CATCHING LEPRECHAUNS

SKILLS   Running; dodging; swerving; hand agility

EQUIPMENT   Small, light hula hoops

FORMATION   A third of the students are leprechaun catchers and are holding hula hoops; the remaining players are leprechauns.

DESCRIPTION

> Because this is a catching game, students need to play somewhat gently. Emphasize having fun with friends, not playing against each other.

> Catchers run after leprechauns, trying to place their hula hoops over their heads. Throwing is not allowed.

> Catchers should try to bring the hula hoops all the way to the hips so as not to choke players around the neck.

> When catching someone, the catcher immediately lets go of the hoop to prevent injuries.

> Leprechauns that are caught become catchers and have to chase someone other than the one who caught them. No tag-backs.

> Leprechauns cannot throw themselves on the ground to avoid being caught. They also cannot push the hula hoop away with their hands. Emphasize the strategies of running and dodging.

TIP   As soon as a leprechaun sees or feels a hula hoop around her body, she should stop running to avoid injury or choking.

ALL FOR ONE

SKILLS Cooperation; hitting; eye–hand coordination; open-movement exploration

EQUIPMENT One beach ball; two cones; three obstacles (e.g., a line of cones, hula hoops, a tunnel)

FORMATION

> ➤ One player stands at one end of the area, between two cones, and with a beach ball.
> ➤ The remaining players spread around the area in front of that player waiting for his kick.
> ➤ The three obstacles are placed opposite the starting player.

DESCRIPTION Be sure to teach your students this game; it brings out the best in them in terms of cooperative feelings and often results in hugs, cheering, and smiles.

> ➤ The starting player kicks the ball, trying to make it go up.
> ➤ The remaining players try to keep the ball in the air until the starter runs to the other side of the field, performs the three obstacles, and runs back to the starting point.
> ➤ If successful, the entire group scores a point and another player is up.
> ➤ Each player gets a second attempt if the first one fails—that is, if the class drops the ball or the initial kick does not go well.
> ➤ The game continues until everyone has had a turn, or until time is up.

2 + 2 ICE CREAM

SKILLS   Creative thinking; running

EQUIPMENT   Small foam noodles; rubber chickens; beanbags (or another type of small equipment they can hold in their hands while playing)

FORMATION

> Four taggers hold short foam noodles (or empty water bottles).
> Other players scatter around and hold a chicken in one hand and a beanbag in the other.

DESCRIPTION   This game was adapted from one my students made up during Making Up Games Week. I find it a tremendous example of second-grade creativity.

> Taggers try to touch a player's hand, either the one holding the chicken or the one holding the beanbag.
> If the tagger tags the hand with the chicken, the tagger gives the player a simple math problem (e.g., 10–7, 2+17).
> If the tagger tags the hand with the beanbag, the tagger requires a compound word (e.g., ice cream, rubber band).
> If the player fails to answer correctly and quickly (in about 10 seconds), the tagger give the player a simple task to perform, such as five jumping jacks, one lap around the room, three push-ups, or five chicken dances.
> Switch taggers every few minutes.

CHAPTER

8

My Vacation Stories

When I meet teenagers who were students of mine from kindergarten through third grade, I often ask them to recall one thing we did in physical education classes, or I ask them what was most memorable to them. Generally, they say something such as "The time we wrestled gorillas in Africa," or "When we were flying hanging on to geese wings."

Every year, after one of the weeklong vacations, I come back with a new Mr. Dienstmann's Amazing and True Vacation Adventure. After convincing the students that teachers have incredibly interesting and fun vacations, I explain that I will be giving them the unbelievable opportunity to act out everything I experienced on my vacation.

The goal of this activity is to explore the widest variety of locomotor, manipulative, and stability experiences through a sequence of small actions belonging to a full action story. The students act out every sequence using their own interpretations of the facts, unless specified. Two short examples follow.

AMAZING AND TRUE VACATION ADVENTURE 1

Every line depicts one movement, exercise, or skill for students to perform. Provide enough time after each line for students to act it out, although not too much time. Tell the story with enthusiasm, but keep good control of the class. Have fun.

- ➤ I decided to go for a run.
- ➤ But I started a bit too fast and got cramps in my legs.
- ➤ I had to do some stretching.
- ➤ I started running again, but my legs were a little stiff and I kept losing my balance.
- ➤ So I decided to lie down with my legs up, and I fell asleep like that.
- ➤ I woke up all stiff and had to go back home walking all bent over like a gorilla.
- ➤ An ambulance drove by; they thought I was cuckoo and took me to a nut house.
- ➤ Because I'm not cuckoo, I escaped during the night by rolling under all the beds,
- ➤ climbing over a tall fence,
- ➤ jumping over a barbed wire fence, and
- ➤ swimming across a river.
- ➤ They sent ferocious dogs after me.
- ➤ I found this wild horse on a field and jumped on and galloped away.
- ➤ I galloped for a whole day until I was completely lost in the forest.
- ➤ It was night again, it was dark . . . I got down from my horse.
- ➤ I was walking alone. I was afraid. I heard things flying over my head [students may portray flying creatures],
- ➤ things crawling around very fast,
- ➤ large frogs jumping around.

- ➤ I saw large crocodiles coming up out of the water to check me out and going back under [students do push-ups].
- ➤ I was shaking; I couldn't control myself.
- ➤ So I climbed a tree, hung onto a rope, and swung away from tree to tree.
- ➤ Then, oops . . . I grabbed on to a snake instead of a rope and fell to the ground.

- I wrestled with this huge snake [bring out jump ropes].
- I finally tamed the snake and jumped rope with it.
- I threw the snake away [throw jump rope aside] and decided to run as fast as I could out of the forest.
- I found a boat in a river; I got in and started rowing.
- I saw some tents by the river. I went into the tents, and the people fed me and told me they were part of a traveling circus.
- They asked me to show them all the gymnastics I know.
- Then they asked me to show them everything I could do with a ball [bring out foam balls],
- with a jump rope [bring out jump rope again],
- and with hula hoops [bring out hula hoops].
- They asked me to show them movements and exercises to perform with a partner.
- After that, they liked me so much that they asked me to join the circus.
- I stayed for a couple of days, but I got tired of it.
- So, I borrowed one of their elephants to travel back home.
- I paraded through town, riding my elephant, with police cars, helicopters, and hundreds of people cheering and dancing after me.
- I got back home safe and sound.

AMAZING AND TRUE VACATION ADVENTURE 2

- It all started when I decided to go kayaking [students paddle].
- This large boat raced past me, sending me tumbling into the river.
- I swam to get back to my kayak, but I was chased by a pack of wild salmon!
- I got out of the water and climbed a tree . . . to the very, very tippy top.
- A helicopter went by, and I grabbed onto the bottom of it and went flying and spinning through the sky.

- The helicopter landed in the middle of a field where the Red Sox [or substitute your local sports team] were practicing. They let me play with them.
- They told me I was not good enough to play with them and sent me away.
- I found an old bike and rode it to the train station.
- I got on the train, and as it moved away, I realized I had no money. They threw me off the train.
- I fell in a pool of quicksand and began to sink.
- This horse was going by, and I grabbed onto its tail and it pulled me out of the quicksand.
- So I climbed onto this beautiful horse and galloped away, jumping over fences and galloping extremely fast.
- But the horse didn't want to stop and carried me all the way to the mountains, where it was cold and snowing.
- I finally jumped off the horse and saw a snowboard lying on the ground.
- I snowboarded down the mountain.
- I fell through a hole and ended up in a scary cave.
- The ceiling of the cave was so low that I had to crawl.
- Some places I had to slither facedown, faceup, and sideways.
- I ended up in a large open space in the cave surrounded by cavemen exercising to become strong [students do push-ups, sit-ups, any exercises they come up with to become strong].
- They thought I was an alien, and I had to act like one.
- When they went to sleep, I finally found an exit and ran away through the forest.
- I found a pack of wild chickens. I tied a couple of chickens on my ankles and a couple of chickens on my wrists and made them fly me back home.
- But they got tired and dropped me in the river in the middle of a bunch of crocodiles.
- I stood on a crocodile and went surfing down the river until I found my kayak again.
- I paddled safely back home.

Index

Note: An italicized *t* following a page number denotes a table.

About the Author

Ronald Dienstmann, ME, is a physical education teacher in Topsfield, Massachusetts. Mr. Dienstmann has been teaching for 25 years and coached for 10 years. A native of Brazil, he spent 10 years working with a Brazilian professor who is a prominent children's swimming education expert. Mr. Dienstmann's work with that professor spurred his interest in the research on emotions and learning and on the schema theory of discrete motor skill learning, which led to the creation of this book.

In his leisure time, Mr. Dienstmann enjoys long-distance biking, reading philosophy, and listening to classical music.

You'll find other outstanding
physical education resources at
www.HumanKinetics.com

In the U.S. call 1.800.747.4457
Australia 08 8372 0999
Canada. 1.800.465.7301
Europe . . . . . +44 (0) 113 255 5665
New Zealand . . . 0064 9 448 1207

HUMAN KINETICS
The Information Leader in Physical Activity
P.O. Box 5076 • Champaign, IL 61825-5076